FOSSIL FISH
FOUND *ALIVE*

DISCOVERING THE COELACANTH

SALLY M. WALKER

CAROLRHODA BOOKS, INC./MINNEAPOLIS

7\02

In memory of my father,
Donald MacArt, a
teller of many great fish
stories, and to my mother,
Cleo Crooks MacArt,
for giving me the rock-
solid base from which I
reach for the stars
—S. M. W.

ACKNOWLEDGMENTS

Coelacanth fever doesn't only strike ichthyologists. Those of us from other walks of life also feel the heat. My swim through the wealth of coelacanth literature has been a fascinating journey, and I couldn't have done it without the help of the coelacanthophiles who kindly threw me a life preserver when I floundered. For answering my many questions, special thanks go to Marjorie Courtenay-Latimer, Karen Hissmann, Mark Erdmann, Samantha Weinberg, and last, but not least, Robin Stobbs, an incredibly patient question-answerer who retired in the 1990s from the J. L. B. Smith Institute of Ichthyology. A grateful nod also to the late Professor James Yolton for introducing me to coelacanths, many years ago, when I was his student.
—S. M. W.

The publisher gratefully acknowledges the assistance of Robin Stobbs, formerly of the J. L. B. Smith Institute of Ichthyology, and James E. Craddock of the Woods Hole Oceanographic Institution.

Carolrhoda Books, Inc.
A division of Lerner Publishing Group
241 First Avenue North
Minneapolis, MN 55401 U.S.A.

Website address: www.lernerbooks.com

Library of Congress Cataloging-in-Publication Data

Walker, Sally M.
    Fossil fish found alive : discovering the coelacanth / by Sally M. Walker.
        p.   cm.
    Includes bibliographical references and index.
    Summary: Describes the 1938 discovery of the coelacanth, a fish previously believed to be extinct,
and subsequent research about it.
    ISBN: 1–57505–536–8 (lib. bdg. : alk. paper)
    1. Coelacanth—Juvenile literature. [1. Coelacanth. 2. Living fossils.] I. Title.
QL638.L26 W36 2002
597.3'9—dc21   2001003815

Manufactured in the United States of America
1 2 3 4 5 6 – JR – 07 06 05 04 03 02

CONTENTS

A PREHISTORIC FISH

It is seventy million years ago on Earth. Deep in a leafy forest, a tiny, shrewlike mammal leaps at a flower and snaps up a nectar-sipping butterfly. A passing triceratops glances at the mammal and looks away. It's more interested in browsing on the leaves that hang across its path.

TRICERATOPS

Suddenly the earth-pounding approach of a tyrannosaur echoes through the forest. The shrewlike mammal heads for cover, and the triceratops moves farther into the underbrush. High in the sky, a pterosaur wings its way over the trees. Unconcerned about the huge predator below, it glides on warm air currents, on the lookout for a quick meal.

In the warm ocean waters far from the forest, life is very different. A plesiosaur swims at a shallow depth. From time to time, its narrow head and long neck break the surface, snaking up into the air. A mosasaur paddles after a small fish, swimming swiftly with its strong flippers. Even the larger, sharp-toothed ichthyosaur flees from this ferocious marine reptile.

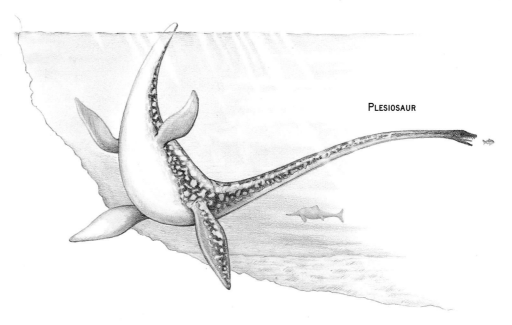

PLESIOSAUR

Several hundred feet below the surface, where the sun's rays barely reach, fish live in a twilight zone. One, a bluish fish with fleshy, rounded fins and an oddly extended tail, lurks in a cave. It seems to hover in the water, resting. Every few seconds, one of the fins on its underside waves gently back and forth.

The fish's kind is almost unthinkably old. Its ancestors swam Earth's oceans, lakes, rivers, and swamps for millions of years before dinosaurs or mammals first walked on land. They hunted the waters for millions of years before pterosaurs first flew the skies. They dwelled in the seas for millions of years before plesiosaurs, mosasaurs, or ichthyosaurs existed. Now, about seventy million years ago, these unusual fish are about to disappear. Like the dinosaurs, pterosaurs, and large marine reptiles, they will become extinct. Or will they?

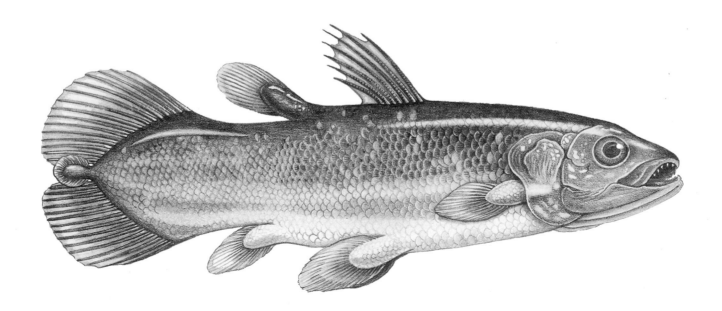

CHAPTER ONE

A STARTLING DISCOVERY

Marjorie Courtenay-Latimer looked closely at the pile of sea creatures in front of her. A flash of blue had caught her eye. She pushed aside a starfish and lifted a small shark. There it was—a beautiful blue fin, glimmering in the sunlight. What kind of fish could it belong to?

It was December 22, 1938. As director of the East London Museum in East London, South Africa, Courtenay-Latimer was responsible for collecting animal and plant specimens for the museum to display. Her friend Hendrik Goosen, captain of the fishing trawler *Nerine,* often gave her fish for the museum from his daily catch. On this visit to his boat, she had seen nothing promising—until now.

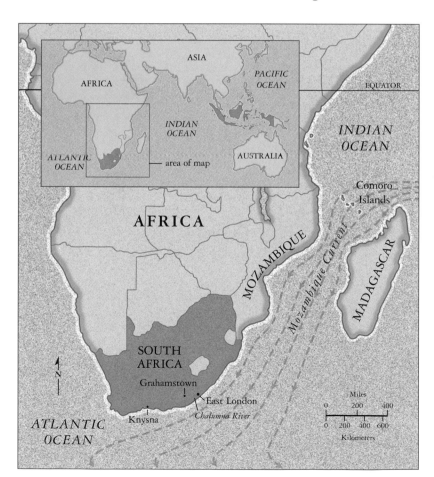

Courtenay-Latimer moved more fish to uncover the creature with the blue fin. "Behold," she recalled, "there appeared the most beautiful fish I had ever seen." Its color was "an iridescent blue with shades of red, green, and brown, with white spots. It was just on five feet long."

Courtenay-Latimer had seen many brightly colored fishes, but this one seemed unusual. It had hard scales covered with spiny points. Its thick tail fin had a strange extension—a smaller fin at the tip that looked like an extra tail. The fish also had four fleshy lower fins, almost like stubby legs with fin-shaped feet. Courtenay-Latimer had never seen a fish like it.

"Yes, miss, it is a strange fish," said the crewman who had helped her board the *Nerine*. "I have been trawling for over thirty years, but I have never seen its like. It snapped at the captain's fingers as he looked at it in the trawl net."

Thinking the fish might be something special, Courtenay-Latimer decided to bring it to the museum. After photographing the fish, she and her assistant, Enoch, put it in a cloth sack, hauled it to a waiting taxi, and loaded it into the trunk. At the museum, Courtenay-Latimer looked through her fish guides, hoping to identify her curious discovery. As she paged through her books, she took a closer look at the fish's hard, spiny scales. Where had she heard of scales like these before?

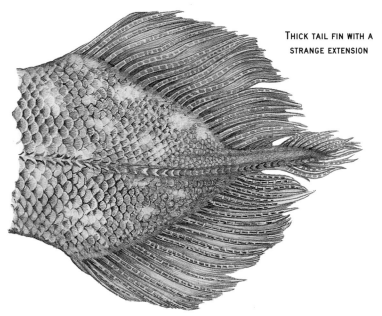

THICK TAIL FIN WITH A STRANGE EXTENSION

Then she remembered. As a student, she had learned that certain fossil fishes—ancient, extinct fishes that are known to scientists only through their fossils—had hard, spiny scales. Studies of the fossil record had revealed that fish first appeared on Earth about 510 million years ago—280 million years before the dinosaurs. The earliest fishes gradually evolved into many different types. One group had hard, spiny scales like the specimen Captain Goosen had caught.

Courtenay-Latimer began to read more about fossil fishes. Some of the descriptions she read sounded very much like her fish. But these fishes were all extinct, and her specimen had been alive several hours before! To solve the puzzle, she would have to ask an ichthyologist—an expert on fishes—to look at the fish. First, though, she had to preserve it. The temperature was very hot, and there were no air conditioners in East London in the 1930s. Before long her fish would begin to rot.

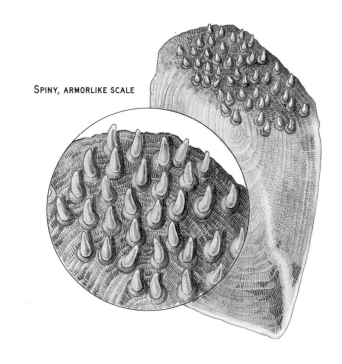

SPINY, ARMORLIKE SCALE

The town had only two refrigerators large enough to store a five-foot fish. Courtenay-Latimer and Enoch loaded the fish into a handcart and wheeled it down the sidewalk. First they tried the hospital morgue, where the director said, "No! Most definitely no!" Next they visited a cold-storage facility used for keeping food. There, too, the manager took a look at the fish and said no.

Since Courtenay-Latimer had no way to keep her fish cool, she took it to Robert Center. He was a taxidermist, a person who stuffs and mounts an animal's remains so it looks alive. Center couldn't work on her fish right away. He and Courtenay-Latimer wrapped it in newspaper and strips of a torn bedsheet soaked with formalin, a liquid used to keep remains from rotting. Their supply of formalin was small, but they hoped it would be enough to preserve the fish for a few days.

Courtenay-Latimer's next task was to find an expert to examine her specimen. She tried to contact J. L. B. Smith, a chemistry professor and ichthyologist in Grahamstown, but she couldn't reach him by phone. The next day, she sent him a letter and a drawing of the fish. Days passed without a reply. (Unbeknownst to Courtenay-Latimer, Smith was at his home in Knysna for the holidays.)

By December 27, the fish had turned dark brown and was beginning to spoil. The formalin hadn't seeped through the fish's hard scales. Courtenay-Latimer told Robert Center to skin the specimen and mount it. At least they could save its skin, head, and fins.

EVOLUTION OF ANIMALS,
IN MILLIONS OF
YEARS AGO

510

440

410

360

286

JAWLESS FISHES

FISHES WITH JAWS

DEVONIAN PERIOD
MANY NEW FISHES, INSECTS

REPTILES

EAST LONDON MUSEUM

ALL SPECIMENS AND EXHIBITS FOR
THE MUSEUM TRAVEL FREE BY POST
OR RAIL IF ADDRESSED:
O.H.M.S.
CURATOR, MUSEUM, EAST LONDON.
PHONE 2095.

East London
SOUTH AFRICA.

23rd Dec. 1938.

Dear Dr Smith,

    I had the most queer looking specimen brought to notice yesterday, The Capt of The trawler told me about it so I immediately set off to see the specimen which I had removed to aur Taxidermist as soon as I could. I however have drawn a very rough sketch and am in hopes that you may be able to assist me in classing it.

It was trawled off Chulmna coast at about 40 fathoms.

    It is coated in heavy scales, almost armour like., the fins resemble limbs, and are scaled right up to a fringe of filment.

The Spinous dorsal, has tiny white spines down each filment.

Note drawing inked in in red.

    I would be so pleased if you could let me Know what you think, though I know just how difficult it is from a discription of this kind.

    Wishing you all happiness for the season.

Yours Sincerely.
M. Courtenay-Latimer

REC. 3/1/39
REP. 3/1 4/1 F/38/47

Bony plates.
scales hard forming an armour almost case like.
Teeth small and sparse scattered on hard palate.
caudal fin

Colour Dark grey. black. (uniform)

Length. 4½ ft.

depth of Body 18 inches

depth of tail 12 inches.

length of fins. spinous Dorsal. 8"
Soft Dorsal 9"
Pectoral — 12"
Pelvic — 8"
ANAL — 12"

MARJORIE COURTENAY-LATIMER SENT THIS LETTER AND DETAILED DRAWING TO J. L. B. SMITH TO DESCRIBE HER MYSTERIOUS DISCOVERY.

8 | 213 | 145 | 65 | 56 | 34 | 24 | 5 | 2 | 0

DINOSAURS, SMALL MAMMALS | **LARGE DINOSAURS, BIRDS** | **DINOSAUR EXTINCTION** | **HORSES** | **APES** | **EARLY HUMANS** | **MODERN HUMANS**

Center cut through the hard scales and into the fish's oily flesh. As he sliced toward the fish's back, Courtenay-Latimer observed that it had no ribs and, instead of a backbone, only a flexible tube. That was unusual—she had expected to see a bony spine. When Center cut through the tube, pale yellow oil flowed out. What kind of fish would be so full of oil? Courtenay-Latimer collected a small bottle of the liquid to give to Smith.

On January 3, 1939, Courtenay-Latimer received a telegram from Smith. She was relieved to hear from him at last—but she quickly became upset. He wanted her to save the fish's internal organs. She didn't have them! At first, Robert Center had kept them, but after several hot days, they had spoiled so badly that he had to throw them away. Courtenay-Latimer tried to search the local garbage dump, but she found that all of East London's garbage was dumped into the ocean. Another disappointing loss was the roll of film containing the photographs of the specimen. The developer had dropped it and ruined the entire roll.

During the next few weeks, the ichthyologist and the museum curator wrote several letters to each other and talked on the telephone. Courtenay-Latimer also sent Smith a sample of the fish's scales. Smith wanted very much to see the fish for himself, but because of work commitments, he wouldn't be able to get to the museum until mid-February. After weeks of waiting, Courtenay-Latimer could do nothing but wait a little longer.

SMITH'S THEORY

While Marjorie Courtenay-Latimer waited in East London, J. L. B. Smith waited 350 miles (560 km) away in Knysna. His wait was especially hard because he had immediately recognized the fish Courtenay-Latimer had drawn. His first clue was the fins. They appeared to be lobed, or rounded and fleshy, instead of slender and supple like the fins most modern fishes have. The second clue was the tiny tail extension, which no other modern fish possesses. The third was the armorlike scales. As far as Smith was concerned, with a body like this one the mysterious specimen could be nothing but an ancient lobe-finned fish called a coelacanth (SEE-luh-kanth).

Scientists had been studying coelacanths since 1839—but only through their fossils. That year, Louis Agassiz, a Swiss naturalist, described a fossil fish found in England and named it *Coelacanthus granulatus*. *Coelacanthus* comes from two Greek words meaning "hollow" and "spine" and refers to the fish's hollow fin spines. *Granulatus* describes the grainy texture of the fish's spiny scales.

Over the next century, scientists had found fossils of dozens of species of coelacanths. Smith knew that these fish ranged in length from only 5 inches (13 cm)—just a bit bigger than a minnow—to 20 inches (50 cm). (Since then, scientists have unearthed coelacanth fossils ranging from 2 inches [5 cm] to 10 feet [3 m] in length.) The earliest coelacanth species first appeared about 400 million years ago, while the most recent seemed to have lived about 70 million years ago. According to the fossil record, coelacanths then disappeared completely—or so scientists believed. Could it be that Marjorie Courtenay-Latimer had found a live coelacanth?

Smith mentioned his theory to Courtenay-Latimer and one other scientist, but until he had seen the fish itself, he didn't dare tell anyone else. Every ichthyologist in the world believed that coelacanths had been extinct for 70 million years. If Smith pronounced Courtenay-Latimer's fish a coelacanth and then turned out to be wrong, he would be a scientific laughingstock. His reputation would be ruined. If he was right, however, the discovery would astound the entire scientific community. It would be like finding a live dinosaur.

Although Smith wished he could rush to East London, he had to finish his work in Knysna first. He would just have to be patient. But J. L. B. Smith had caught coelacanth fever. He spent sleepless nights thinking about the fish, and the next few weeks seemed like years.

IDENTIFIED!

On February 16, eight weeks after the fish had been caught, Smith finally walked into the East London Museum. He was almost afraid to look at the fish. If his theory was right, neither his life nor the study of fish would ever be the same.

Courtenay-Latimer showed him the mounted fish, which rested on a large table. Smith's legs shook as he walked around it. Slowly, he reached out and petted the fish. All doubt was gone—the fish *was* a coelacanth. Smith turned to Marjorie Courtenay-Latimer and said, "Lass, this discovery will be on the lips of every scientist in the world."

MARJORIE
COURTENAY-LATIMER
AND THE FISH THAT
J. L. B. SMITH
IDENTIFIED AT LAST

CHAPTER TWO

MEET THE COELACANTH

J. L. B. Smith was right. Newspaper headlines all over the globe reported the discovery of the "living fossil." "Loch Ness Outdone," said a New Zealand paper, referring to the legendary sea monster of Scotland. The *London Illustrated News* called the discovery "sensational." Smith received dozens of phone calls and letters from stunned scientists.

Some of the publicity irritated Smith because it was scientifically irresponsible. Certain newspapers, for example, claimed that the coelacanth was the "missing link" between sea animals and land animals—the first fish that developed legs and crept onto land. According to the theory of evolution, all other four-legged land animals—and eventually human beings—evolved from this missing link.

Based on the fossil record, paleontologists believed the missing link evolved from a lobe-finned fish near the end of the Devonian period, a geologic time period that ended about 360 million years ago. Three groups of lobe-finned fishes lived during the Devonian: the rhipidistians, which became extinct about 300 million years ago; the coelacanths, which had been presumed extinct until Courtenay-Latimer's discovery; and the lungfishes, which still live in Africa, Australia, and South America. Scientists had argued for decades over which of these fishes might have given rise to the missing link.

When the coelacanth discovery was announced, some journalists seized on the dramatic idea that the

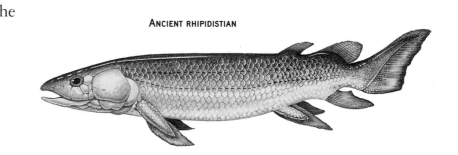

ANCIENT RHIPIDISTIAN

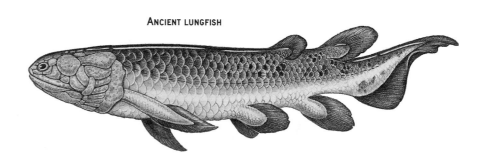

ANCIENT LUNGFISH

coelacanth was the missing link, even though no one had any real evidence to prove this theory. Smith didn't believe the fish that had evolved legs was a coelacanth at all—he thought it was probably one of the other lobe-finned fishes. But many people linked the reports to him anyway. In 1939, the theory of evolution was still a hotly debated idea. The headlines that touted the coelacanth as the missing link angered people who didn't agree with the theory of evolution. Some wrote letters to Smith, accusing him of spreading "evil" ideas.

But most people were simply excited about the amazing discovery. When Marjorie Courtenay-Latimer displayed the coelacanth on February 20, 1939, thousands of people flocked to the East London Museum to see it. After its display at the museum, the coelacanth was sent under police guard to Smith's home so he could study and photograph it. He could hardly wait to undertake the important tasks that lay ahead. For the first time ever, a scientist could study a real coelacanth, not just a fossil. And Smith was about to choose a name for the most valuable scientific treasure he had ever seen.

In the scientific community, the privilege of naming a newly discovered animal or plant goes to the person who first describes it in a published report. A scientific name has two parts. The first part, the genus, is a group of animals or plants that are alike in certain ways. The second part specifies a particular member of the genus. Together, the two parts make up the species name. Members of the same species look similar to one another and can mate and produce young.

In an article for *Nature*, a well-known scientific journal, Smith described the coelacanth and gave it the name *Latimeria chalumnae*. *Latimeria*, the genus, honors Marjorie Courtenay-Latimer's discovery of the fish. Smith named the species *chalumnae* because Hendrik Goosen had caught it near the mouth of the Chalumna River.

SCALES, FINS, AND HOLES

After naming the coelacanth, Smith began an intensive examination of its body. Many crucial parts were missing, but he was able to study the skin closely. He removed several scales and looked at them with a microscope. Although most fishes have smooth scales, only the lower half of the coelacanth's scales was smooth. Toothlike spines called denticles covered the upper half of each scale, making it rough and scratchy, like sandpaper. The smooth lower half of each scale was protected by the denticles of the two scales that overlapped it. Smith theorized that these rough, layered scales provided armorlike protection against predators and the rough edges of rocks.

Like the fossil coelacanths that scientists had studied, this fish had several lobed fins, including two pectoral fins near the head and two pelvic fins on the belly.

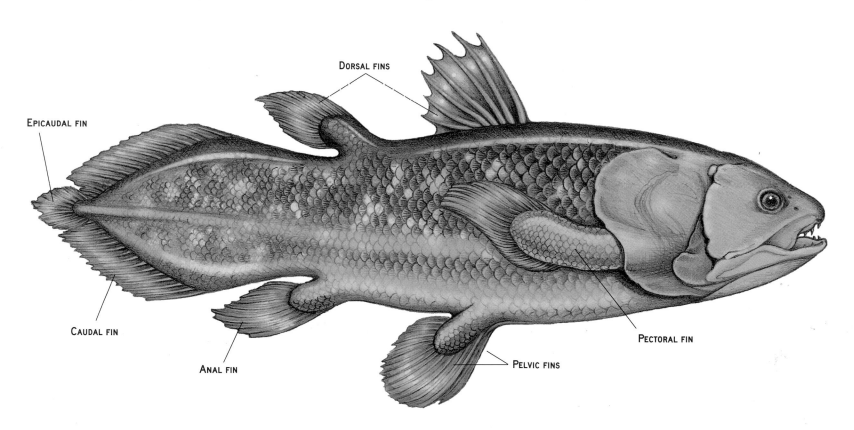

DORSAL FINS

EPICAUDAL FIN

CAUDAL FIN

ANAL FIN

PELVIC FINS

PECTORAL FIN

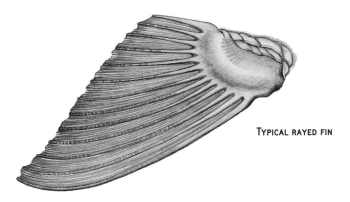

TYPICAL RAYED FIN

LOBED FIN

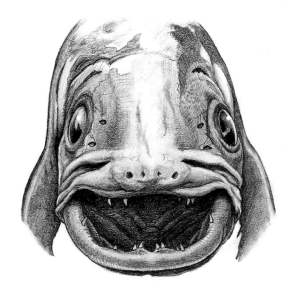

SIX SMALL OPENINGS IN HEAD;
TWO NOSTRILS IN CENTER OF SNOUT

Unlike the rayed fins that most fishes have, the lobed fins had a rounded, fleshy base that stuck out from the fish's body. To Smith, these two pairs of lobed fins resembled stubby legs with fins instead of feet. Perhaps, he wrote, coelacanths could "stalk [other fishes] by crawling quietly along gullies and channels, pressing close against the rocks for added concealment." Of course, Smith couldn't prove this idea since no one had seen the coelacanth move underwater.

Smith studied the coelacanth's large tail fin, known to ichthyologists as the caudal fin, for hours. He was especially intrigued by the tiny "extra" tail—the epicaudal fin—that protruded from the caudal fin. No other modern fish has an epicaudal fin. Smith wondered if it helped the coelacanth swim. If not, what did it do?

A new mystery appeared when Smith examined the coelacanth's head. He could clearly see six small holes—two near each eye and two toward the tip of the snout. These holes had never been observed in a coelacanth fossil. They looked like nostrils, but they weren't connected to the fish's smelling system. Instead, the holes led to a space in the coelacanth's head. This cavity wasn't located where the coelacanth's brain had been. Smith had never seen anything like the holes or the cavity in a living fish. He thought they might be part of a sensory system. But how did the fish use them?

The coelacanth thrilled J. L. B. Smith, but he wasn't satisfied with looking at scales and fins. Studying a stuffed coelacanth was like having only a few pieces of a puzzle. Smith had so many unanswered questions. How did the coelacanth use its four leglike fins? What were its internal organs like? How did it find food? To complete the puzzle, he needed another coelacanth—but where should he look?

TO FIND A FISH

Smith thought about the place where Hendrik Goosen had caught the coelacanth—the ocean waters near the Chalumna River. He didn't think this heavily fished area was the coelacanth's natural habitat. If it was, fishers certainly would have caught one before.

After the publication of Smith's *Nature* article, scientist E. I. White suggested that coelacanths must have been hiding for millions of years in very deep water. Smith disagreed. He had seen fishes that lived at great depths. Their bodies were soft and fragile. The coelacanth was a sturdy fish with strong scales. It had survived for hours in Captain Goosen's net, even though the bodies of other fishes had pressed tightly on top of it. It surely lived in only moderately deep water, near rocks where it could walk about on its four lobed fins.

If the coelacanth didn't live near the Chalumna River or in deeper water farther from the coast, where was its home? Smith knew that a warm current called the Mozambique Current flowed southward along the southeastern coast of Africa. He felt sure this current had carried the coelacanth from moderately deep waters hundreds of miles to the north. For now, though, the coelacanth's home was still a mystery—like so many other things about it.

CHAPTER THREE

A FOURTEEN-YEAR FISH HUNT

PREMIO   £ 100   REWARD
RÉCOMPENSE

Examine este peixe com cuidado. Talvez lhe dê sorte. Repare nos dois rabos que possui e nas suas estranhas barbatanas. O único exemplar que a ciência encontrou tinha, de comprimento, 160 centímetros. Mas já houve quem visse outros. Se tiver a sorte de apanhar ou encontrar algum NÃO O CORTE NEM O LIMPE DE QUALQUER MODO — conduza-o imediatamente, inteiro, a um frigorífico ou peça a pessoa competente que dele se ocupe. Solicite, ao mesmo tempo, a essa pessoa, que avise imediatamente, por meio de telgrama o professor J. L. B. Smith, da Rhodes University, Grahamstown, União Sul-Africana.
Os dois primeiros especimes serão pagos à razão de 10.000$, cada, sendo o pagamento garantido pela Rhodes University e pelo South African Council for Scientific and Industrial Research. Se conseguir obter mais de dois, conserve-os todos, visto terem grande valor, para fins científicos, e as suas canseiras serão bem recompensadas.

COELACANTH

Look carefully at this fish. It may bring you good fortune. Note the peculiar double tail, and the fins. The only one ever saved for science was 5 ft (160 cm.) long. Others have been seen. If you have the good fortune to catch or find one DO NOT CUT OR CLEAN IT ANY WAY but get it whole at once to a cold storage or to some responsible official who can care for it, and ask him to notify Professor J. L. B. Smith of Rhodes University Grahamstown, Union of S. A., immediately by telegraph. For the first 2 specimens £100 (10.000 Esc.) each will be paid, guaranteed by Rhodes University and by the South African Council for Scientific and Industrial Research. If you get more than 2, save them all, as every one is valuable for scientific purposes and you will be well paid.

Veuillez remarquer avec attention ce poisson. Il pourra vous apporter bonne chance, peut être. Regardez les deux queues qu'il possède et ses étranges nageoires. Le seul exemplaire que la science a trouvé avait, de longueur, 160 centimètres. Cependant d'autres ont trouvés quelques exemplaires en plus. Si jamais vous avez la chance d'en trouver un NE LE DÉCOUPEZ PAS NI NE LE NETTOYEZ D'AUCUNE FAÇON, conduisez-le immediatement, tout entier, a un frigorifique ou glacière en demandat a une personne competente de s'en occuper. Simultanement veuillez prier a cette personne de faire part telegraphiquement à Mr. le Professeus J. L. B. Smith, de la Rhodes University, Grahamstown, Union Sud-Africaine. Le deux premiers exemplaires seront payés a la raison de £ 100 chaque dont le payment est garanti par la Rhodes University et par le South African Council for Scientific and Industrial Research. Si, jamais il vous est possible d'en obtenir plus de deux, nous vous serions très grés de les conserver vu qu'ils sont d'une très grande valeur pour fins scientifiques, et, neanmoins les fatigues pour obtantion seront bien recompensées.

J. L. B. SMITH'S REWARD LEAFLET OFFERED GOOD FORTUNE FOR COELACANTH HUNTERS IN THREE LANGUAGES.

After J. L. B. Smith returned the coelacanth to the East London Museum in May 1939, he couldn't stop thinking about finding a second specimen. Someone, somewhere, must have caught another coelacanth. He talked with hundreds of fishers in southern Africa, but no one could help him.

While Smith sought the coelacanth's home, tension was growing between nations in Europe and Asia. World War II began in September 1939. As the fighting grew more intense, most scientists focused on the war effort. Smith wasn't healthy enough to serve in the army, so he continued his university teaching in chemistry. But he didn't forget the coelacanth. It had become his obsession.

Working with his wife, Margaret, Smith kept up the search. The Smiths walked hundreds of miles, visiting wharves throughout South Africa. They told the coelacanth's story and gave out copies of its photograph. Sometimes they heard about fish that sounded much like a coelacanth. But no one had taken any photographs or saved the bodies.

After the war ended in 1945, Smith began work on a book about South African fishes. And he came up with a new plan to find a coelacanth: offering a reward. He raised money and printed leaflets that described the coelacanth in Portuguese, French, and English. The leaflet promised one hundred pounds—a substantial sum of money—for each of the first two specimens found. As the Smiths conducted research for J. L. B.'s book, they distributed the leaflets all along the southeastern coast of Africa. Years went by, but still no one reported catching a coelacanth.

HUNT'S HUNT

In 1952, a friend of the Smiths introduced Margaret to a trader who shared the Smiths' interest in unusual fish. Eric Hunt often collected specimens for his home aquarium. When he learned of the Smiths' search for the coelacanth, he asked one question after another. Then he asked a question that J. L. B. Smith had already considered himself: Could the fish live in the Comoro Islands?

The Comoro Islands are a group of small islands several hundred miles off the coast of East Africa. Because the Smiths had searched almost every other possible location, J. L. B. had thought that the reefs around these islands might be the coelacanth's home. But it would take time and a large boat to go there, and the Smiths had never managed to make the trip. Eric Hunt, however, frequently visited the Comoro Islands to trade. He agreed to take a handful of coelacanth leaflets along on his next trip and arranged for a shipment of formalin to be sent to the Comoro Islands in case a specimen was caught.

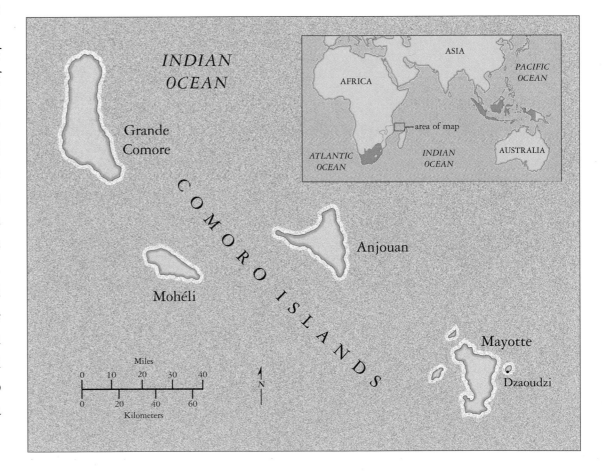

Several weeks later, Margaret Smith ran into Hunt again. True to his word, he had already begun sharing J. L. B.'s reward leaflets with Comoran fishers. Now he wondered what he should do if someone caught a coelacanth before his shipment of formalin arrived. Margaret suggested that he rub the fish with salt. Hunt told Margaret that he would send the Smiths a telegram when he had his coelacanth. They both had to laugh at his confidence. After all, how likely was it that he would find a fish no one else had found for fourteen years?

A Comoran Fish

On the night of December 20, 1952—less than a week after Eric Hunt and Margaret Smith spoke—a Comoran fisher named Ahamadi Abdallah sat in a dugout canoe, fighting a fish. Abdallah had hooked the creature moments before in water about 520 feet (160 m) deep. It wasn't easy to see in the dark, and the fish fought hard, but he got it up out of the water at last. He clubbed the fish on its head and killed it. Abdallah recognized it as a fish the Comorans called *gombessa.* Though he knew it would be too oily to taste good, he brought his catch home as he always did.

The next morning, Abdallah lugged the strange fish onto the beach near his home. He sat poised to clean and gut it. Suddenly a voice called to him to stop his work. It was Affane Mohamed, a teacher who had just gotten a shave and a haircut near Abdallah's home. He had heard about Abdallah's unusual catch and decided to investigate. As soon as he saw the fish, Mohamed was sure he had seen it before—on a poster from the trader Eric Hunt. He brought the fish to Hunt to find out.

Like J. L. B. Smith, Hunt had caught coelacanth fever after hearing the story of the ancient fish. He had gazed at the fish's photograph long enough to know exactly what the Comoran fisher had caught. By this time, a day had passed since Abdallah had caught the fish, and it was starting to rot. But Hunt had not yet received his shipment of formalin. Remembering Margaret Smith's advice, he had his crew cut the fish open and salt its internal organs to preserve them. Next he sailed with the fish to the town of Dzaoudzi, where he got some formalin from a doctor and began to compose a very important telegram.

THE SECOND COELACANTH

While Eric Hunt worked in Dzaoudzi, the Smiths were sailing home after a fish-collecting expedition. On December 24, their

HUNT AND HIS CREW ABOARD HIS SCHOONER, THE *N'DUWARO*. ABDALLAH'S CATCH IS IN THE BOX AT LOWER LEFT.

ship docked for Christmas Eve. J. L. B. Smith received several telegrams, including one marked "urgent":

HAVE FIVE FOOT SPECIMEN COELACANTH INJECTED FORMALIN HERE KILLED TWENTIETH ADVISE REPLY HUNT DZAOUDZI.

A coelacanth at last—but how would Smith reach it? He learned that Dzaoudzi was a small village near the Comoran island of Mayotte. His fish was hundreds of miles away! It had been caught four days earlier, on December 20, and the weather was extremely hot—just like it was when Marjorie Courtenay-Latimer found her fish. Even though Hunt had injected the specimen with formalin, it might be in danger of rotting.

Smith's mind raced. He had to get to Dzaoudzi as soon as possible. Traveling by boat was out of the question—it would take too long. He needed to go by airplane, but he couldn't just hop on a flight to the Comoros. No airline flew there from South Africa in 1952.

For a short time Smith was stumped. Then he picked up the telephone and got busy. The only available planes belonged to the South African government, so Smith called several government officials. He had no luck. Their offices were closed for the holidays. "Why on earth did coelacanths want to turn up just before Christmas?" Smith wondered. He even tried calling the officials at their homes, but many were away on vacation. The people he did speak with didn't have the authority to lend him a plane.

Desperate, Smith phoned the armed forces, but his request was flatly refused. The Comoro Islands were a French colony. The South African military couldn't send a flight into foreign territory on such short notice.

The day after Christmas, another telegram came from Eric Hunt:

CHARTER PLANE IMMEDIATELY   AUTHORITIES TRYING TO CLAIM SPECIMEN BUT WILLING TO LET YOU HAVE IT IF IN PERSON STOP   PAID FISHERMAN REWARD TO STRENGTHEN POSITION STOP   INSPECTED [PROBABLY A MISPRINT OF "INJECTED"] FIVE KILO FORMALIN   NO REFRIGERATOR STOP   SPECIMEN DIFFERENT YOURS   NO FRONT DORSAL OR TAIL REMNANT BUT DEFINITE IDENTIFICATION   HUNT.

If the French government claimed the coelacanth, Smith would never get to examine it at all. He realized that Prime Minister D. F. Malan, the head of South Africa's government, was the only person who could authorize a plane at such short notice. But calling Malan made him uneasy. Malan didn't think much of the British—and Smith was British. Even worse, Malan's religion taught that the theory of evolution was wrong. Why would he want to help a British scientist retrieve a fish that some people had called a missing link in the history of evolution? But Smith had no choice. If he wanted that fish, Prime Minister Malan was his last chance.

Since Smith didn't know Malan, he asked Vernon Shearer, a local government official, to telephone him. Malan's wife answered. She told them her husband had gone to bed—it was after ten o'clock at night—and she wouldn't disturb him. Smith was devastated. Now he was sure his coelacanth would rot, just as the first one had.

Half an hour later, the Shearers' telephone rang. It was the prime minister! He had heard the phone ring earlier and had asked his wife about the call. Malan had read and admired Smith's book about South African fishes. He figured that Smith would only have called so late about something extremely important.

Nervously, Smith told his story. He explained how urgent it was to bring the coelacanth to South Africa. A complete specimen would bring the nation scientific prestige. He also acknowledged that the fish Hunt had found might

THE AIR FORCE DAKOTA
THAT CARRIED J. L. B.
SMITH TO HIS FISH. SMITH
STANDS THIRD FROM THE
LEFT; ERIC HUNT IS
SECOND FROM LEFT.

not be a coelacanth—but he believed it was. To Smith's relief, Malan agreed to authorize a plane. Soon Smith would be with his fish.

HUNT'S CATCH

Just after dawn on December 28, Smith and the crew of an air force Dakota took off for the Comoro Islands. Smith was ready—he had two gallons of formalin in his luggage. The pilot was mostly ready—he didn't know if the islands had a landing strip where he could set down his plane. As they flew, icy air blew in through the ventilation holes drilled in the plane's unlined hull.

After an overnight stop on Mozambique Island, the Dakota approached the Comoro Islands at last. Dark clouds filled the sky, but the pilot spotted a small airstrip. Smith saw a schooner floating in the harbor. He realized it probably belonged to Eric Hunt. Somewhere on that boat, his coelacanth was waiting.

The plane landed in pouring rain. When the Dakota's door opened, Smith saw Eric Hunt looking in at him. "Where's the fish?" Smith cried. He was ready to rush to the wharf, but Hunt stopped him. While Smith was on his way, Hunt had been busy keeping the Comoran authorities happy. He had persuaded them to let Smith have the fish rather than give it to the French government. But now Smith had to be polite. The islands' governor wanted to meet them and go with them to the wharf.

Reluctantly, Smith visited the governor, who had food and drinks waiting. Smith was so excited he couldn't eat. "Blast those formalities!" he recalled. "I wanted only one thing, and that was to see the fish, to know if I was a fool or a prophet." Unable to wait a minute longer, he finally asked if they could please get in the car and go see the fish.

A large wooden box rested on the deck of Hunt's schooner, the *N'duwaro*. Hunt pulled open the lid. When the covering was lifted off the fish, Smith immediately saw the familiar spiny scales and lobed fins. He was so overcome he couldn't speak. "It was a coelacanth all right," he recalled. "I knelt down on the deck so as to get a closer view, and as I caressed that fish I found tears splashing on my hands and realized that I was weeping, and was quite without shame. Fourteen of the best years of my life had gone in this search and it was true; it was really true. It had come at last."

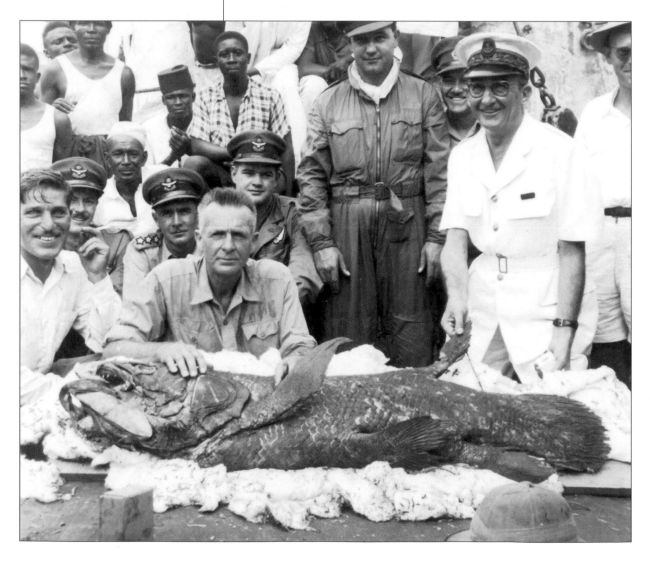

CHAPTER FOUR

INSIDE THE COELACANTH

J. L. B. Smith's worries were not over. It still seemed possible that the French government might claim the coelacanth as its own, since France controlled the Comoros. So he wasted no time in bringing his prize back to South Africa. As the 1939 discovery had, this find made headlines throughout the world. Smith, already exhausted from his quest, was bombarded with phone calls and requests for interviews.

In spite of the strain, Smith quickly submitted a description of the fish to *Nature*. Because this coelacanth had only one dorsal fin and no epicaudal fin, he believed it was a different genus and species than the first. He named it *Malania anjouanae*, in honor of Prime Minister Malan and Anjouan, the island where the fish was caught.

With every publication and observation about the coelacanth, Smith was blazing a new trail in ichthyology. Like many scientific trailblazers, he occasionally made a mistake. This was one such time. Other scientists who later examined the fish determined it wasn't a new genus, and Smith eventually agreed with them. The front dorsal fin and epicaudal fin were only missing, perhaps bitten off by another fish when the coelacanth was young.

SMITH SHOWS THE COELACANTH TO HIS WIFE, MARGARET (RIGHT), AND PRIME MINISTER D. F. MALAN (FAR LEFT).

The discovery of another living coelacanth prompted many people to wonder how scientists could have wrongly assumed for so many years that the fish were extinct. Why had it taken so long for people to find coelacanths if they were alive all the time?

It's impossible to say for certain how coelacanths survived the changes that killed the dinosaurs and many other animals. But people on the Comoro Islands had caught coelacanths prior to 1952. Comorans reported that because the fish don't taste very good, they weren't sought as food—but they were sometimes caught accidentally. It wasn't until Eric Hunt brought J. L. B. Smith's leaflets that anyone there realized the fish's scientific importance.

THE COELACANTH WAS SO VALUABLE TO SMITH THAT HE EVEN SLEPT BESIDE IT.

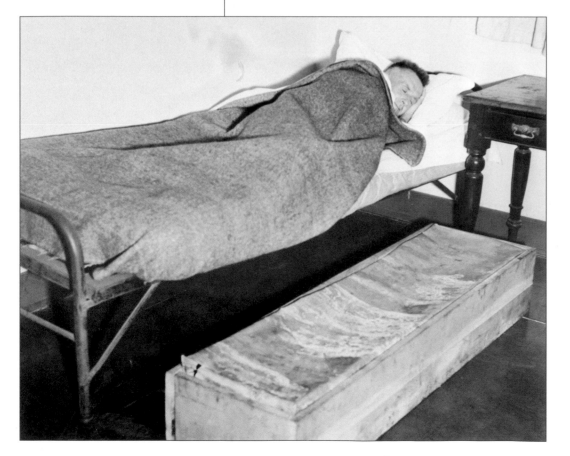

INSIDE THE FISH

After naming his coelacanth, Smith began a methodical study of the fish he had sought for fourteen years. One of the first things he looked for were the six strange holes and the cavity he'd found in the head of Marjorie Courtenay-Latimer's fish. They were there—and in the past fourteen years, they had still never been seen in any other fish. Smith continued to think that coelacanths used the holes for sensing. But once again, he had no way to test his ideas. The unusual holes remained a mystery.

Smith expected that like Marjorie Courtenay-Latimer's coelacanth, his new specimen would have a hollow tube filled with yellow oil instead of a backbone. As he sliced into the fish, he saw that he was right. This interesting structure, called a notochord, is different from the backbones that humans and most other vertebrate animals have. Instead of bone, a notochord is made of cartilage, the flexible, rubbery tissue found in a person's ears and nose. All animals with backbones have a notochord at some point during the early stages of their development. Before birth the notochord is replaced by bony vertebrae, which make up the backbone. Only a few, very primitive animals retain a notochord all their lives.

Inside the specimen's intestines, Smith found two fish eyeballs and some scales, proving that coelacanths hunt other fish for food. Smith also found an intestinal spiral-shaped valve similar to the one that sharks have. This valve allows food to be digested slowly and very completely. Because nutrients are extracted from each meal over a long period of time, a coelacanth—like many types of sharks—can probably go days or weeks without eating again.

A FRENCH FISH

After publishing a detailed description of his coelacanth, J. L. B. Smith hoped to return to the Comoro Islands to hunt for another specimen. The fish he had just studied was a male. Perhaps he could find a female and learn how coelacanths produce young. But many French officials were upset that Smith had taken the fish and that a foreign government's plane had landed in their territory without French permission. To his dismay, Smith was told that only French scientists would be allowed to remove and study any coelacanths caught near the Comoro Islands. Although Smith went on to publish *Old Fourlegs,* a popular 1956 book about his coelacanth discoveries, his role in this scientific drama had largely come to a close.

Meanwhile, French scientists were eager to find and study more coelacanths. Jacques Millot, the scientist placed in charge of this research, shipped a large supply of formalin to the Comoros and urged fishers to save and report any catches. By the end of 1954, five more specimens had been caught and preserved, and many others followed. Millot and other French scientists spent almost twenty years studying these fish. They learned that modern coelacanths can grow to 5.9 feet (1.8 m) long and weigh up to 180 pounds (82 kg)—about the size and weight of a fairly tall adult man.

Several fishers who had caught coelacanths reported that their eyes seemed to glow in the dark. Millot and his colleagues found the explanation for this

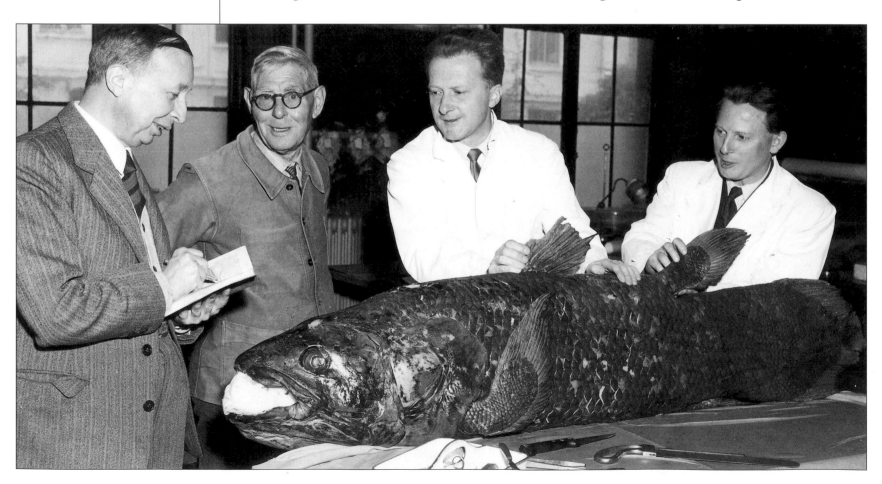

phenomenon in the retina, the part of the eye that senses and reacts to light. A coelacanth's retina contains a layer of cells called a tapetum. The tapetum reflects light back through the retina, so the retina "sees" the light two times instead of just once. When light strikes the tapetum, it makes a coelacanth's eyes glow, like a cat's eyes do when light strikes them in the dark. Millot also observed that a coelacanth's eyes have many rods—tiny structures that help animals see in dim light. Together, the rods and tapetum help the fish see better in dark water.

Another organ the French scientists studied was the swim bladder. In most fishes, this small, balloonlike organ contains gases such as oxygen and nitrogen. Fish are denser than water, so they do not normally float. When a fish needs to maintain a certain depth in the water, gases from its blood pass into its swim bladder. Filled with gas, the swim bladder makes the fish more buoyant, so it

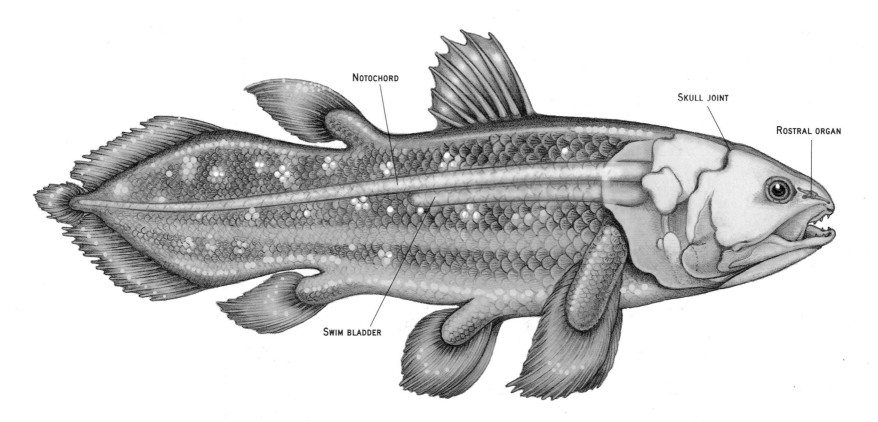

NOTOCHORD

SKULL JOINT

ROSTRAL ORGAN

SWIM BLADDER

doesn't sink. When a fish swims into deeper water, gases pass out of the swim bladder and back into the fish's blood. With less gas, the swim bladder allows the fish to maintain a lower depth.

A coelacanth's swim bladder doesn't work this way. Like several other deep-sea fishes, a coelacanth has a bladder filled with oily, fatty tissue that remains in the bladder at all times. Instead of adjusting to different depths like a gas-filled swim bladder, the fat-filled bladder balances out the density of the fish's bones and tissues without changing. The coelacanth naturally hovers at the same depth underwater unless it actively swims up or down.

Oil and fatty material also fill every tiny space in a coelacanth's bones and muscle tissues. In most fishes, these spaces are air-filled. Like the swim bladder, the oil and fat increase a coelacanth's ability to maintain its position in the water. This body structure helps a coelacanth conserve energy. It doesn't have to work as hard as most other fishes do to stay at any depth it chooses.

INTERNATIONAL INVESTIGATIONS

In the late 1950s, some non-French scientists were permitted to start their own coelacanth studies. A few years later, France began to allow the Comoran government to sell specimens to other countries. Many scientists and natural-history museums asked to purchase a coelacanth. Comoran fishers had no way to target the fish specifically. But they were glad to turn in those they caught by accident because they still received a reward of one hundred pounds—five times the amount most Comorans earned in an entire year—for every specimen. And in the hope of obtaining a live specimen for study, Jacques Millot doubled the reward for a living fish.

Comoran fishers caught about 150 coelacanths between 1952 and 1987. Many were still alive when brought to the surface, and scientists tried various means of saving them. One coelacanth was taken down to the ocean floor and anchored with a rope. Another was placed in a submerged cage, and another in a huge, aquarium-like tank. Despite efforts like these, the fish all died within hours. Coelacanths didn't seem to be able to survive the trip to the surface and exposure to warm water and sunlight. Several expeditions that aimed to capture a live specimen also failed.

Although no one managed to obtain a live coelacanth, the dead specimens allowed scientists to continue answering questions about the fish's biology and way of life. Because methods of preservation had improved since J. L. B. Smith's research, the quality of specimens improved as well. Deep-frozen coelacanths could be shipped to countries far from the Comoro Islands, so scientists worldwide could examine tissues that had not been contaminated with formalin.

Dissection of coelacanth stomachs revealed more about what the fish eat. The stomachs contained fishes such as deep-water snappers and cardinal fish, lantern fish, squid, skates, eels, small sharks, and beardfish. Most had been swallowed whole. Because many of these fishes are active at night, scientists speculated that coelacanths were nocturnal hunters that rested during the day.

Researchers found an intriguing puzzle when they examined the specimens' heads—a strange joint that separates the front part of the skull from the back. Some fossil fishes also had this joint, but except for coelacanths, no modern animals do. What was its purpose?

In 1966, biologist Keith Thomson wondered if the joint might make catching prey easier. He decided to

DIVERS TRY TO REVIVE A COELACANTH ACCIDENTALLY CAUGHT OFF GRANDE COMORE. LIKE OTHER SUCH ATTEMPTS, THIS ONE FAILED.

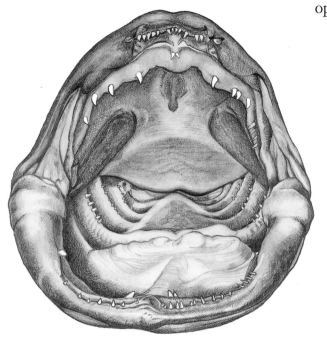

Gaping jaw, front view

open the mouth of a specimen that had been frozen and thawed. Thomson lifted the tip of the coelacanth's snout. As the snout swung upward, the fish's lower jaw pushed prominently forward. The coelacanth's mouth gaped wide open.

The joint, Thomson realized, allows a coelacanth's mouth to open very wide and very quickly. This gaping action creates suction. Thomson theorized that the suction might be strong enough to pull prey toward, or even into, a coelacanth's mouth. Of course, researchers could test this theory only by watching a coelacanth catch its prey. Even decades after the discovery of the first coelacanth in 1938, that still hadn't happened.

Scientists also investigated how long coelacanths live by examining the growth rings in ear bones called otoliths. Like many fishes, coelacanths have otoliths that grow over time. It appears that the fish can live as long as 80 to 100 years.

Another important topic of investigation was how coelacanths produce their young, which are called pups. Some fishes give birth to live

JAW CLOSED

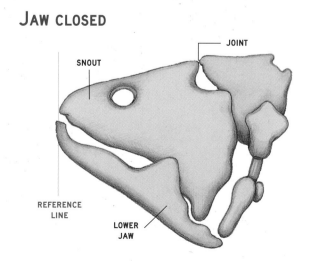

SNOUT

JOINT

REFERENCE LINE

LOWER JAW

JAW OPEN

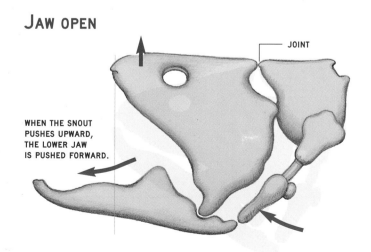

JOINT

WHEN THE SNOUT PUSHES UPWARD, THE LOWER JAW IS PUSHED FORWARD.

young, but most lay eggs. Fossil evidence about ancient coelacanths seemed contradictory. Some fossils showed traces of eggs. But because one fossil showed the skeletons of two small coelacanths within an adult, some paleontologists believed the fish gave birth to live young.

The question seemed to be answered when French scientists found reddish-colored eggs inside a female's body. Most egg-laying fishes lay hundreds or thousands of tiny eggs at a time. In comparison, female coelacanths seemed to produce only a few, very large eggs. One female had nineteen grapefruit-sized eggs in her body, each weighing about three-fourths of a pound. They were the largest fish eggs ever recorded. Clearly, scientists concluded, coelacanths were egg layers—and impressive ones at that.

A dramatic find in 1975 reversed this belief. Scientists dissected a female coelacanth and found five pups inside. None of the pups were inside an egg; they would have been born live had the female lived. This discovery proved that like some sharks and stingrays, coelacanths are ovoviviparous. Each pup begins development inside a membrane-covered egg in the mother's body. As the pup develops, the membrane disappears. The egg's yolk sac remains attached to the pup's stomach, supplying the food the pup needs to grow. When the pups have developed enough to survive, the mother gives birth to live young.

The six strange holes and skull cavity that had baffled J. L. B. Smith continued to puzzle coelacanth researchers for decades. By the 1970s, these features had been examined many times. Scientists had found that each of the six holes was

DISSECTION OF A FEMALE COELACANTH REVEALED THESE EGGS, WHICH HAD NOT YET DEVELOPED TO THEIR FULL SIZE.

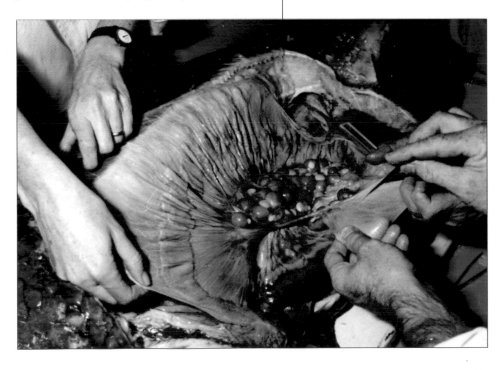

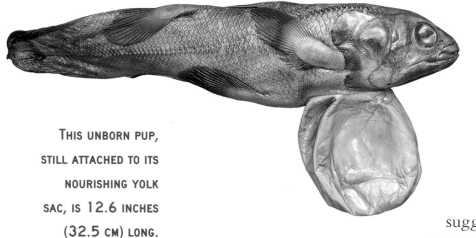

THIS UNBORN PUP, STILL ATTACHED TO ITS NOURISHING YOLK SAC, IS 12.6 INCHES (32.5 CM) LONG.

the outer opening of a tube filled with a jellylike substance. The tubes led into the jelly-filled head cavity. Together the tubes and cavity were named the rostral organ. (The word *rostral* means "toward the nose or mouth.") Most scientists agreed with Smith's early theory that the rostral organ was used for sensing, but no one knew how. Did it sense changes in temperature, chemicals, or something else? Several researchers, beginning as early as 1971, suggested that the rostral organ detects electrical pulses.

All living creatures give off small electrical pulses as their muscles move and as chemicals inside the body react with one another. Although only coelacanths have a rostral organ, many fishes have other means of sensing these pulses. They use this ability to track prey. Perhaps coelacanths do the same thing. The electrical pulses may travel through the jelly-filled tubes into the cavity, where nerves sense them.

In 1987, scientist Bernd Fritzch discovered yet another bizarre coelacanth feature. A coelacanth's ears contain a membrane called a basilar papilla. The presence of this membrane in a fish is very puzzling because it's associated with hearing in air. The ears of all mammals and some amphibians have a basilar papilla. But fish ears do not—except the coelacanth's.

No one knows how the membrane helps a coelacanth function in its underwater home. Was the development of the basilar papilla an early step toward a body suited for living on land? The membrane would have given an ancient land dweller the advantage of being able to hear predators and prey. Did ancient coelacanths actually evolve into land dwellers? Could they be the missing link between land animals and sea animals after all?

As in J. L. B. Smith's time, most modern scientists believe four-legged land dwellers evolved from the extinct rhipidistians, the lungfishes, or the coelacanths. Although coelacanths share some characteristics with early land dwellers, lungfishes share more. So while many scientists believe coelacanths are distantly related to the first fish that walked out of the sea, few think they are the missing link.

Fossils of the common ancestor shared by the three groups of lobe-finned fishes have not yet been found. Perhaps they contain clues that could help solve this puzzle. And tests conducted in 1991 showed that coelacanths seem to be more closely related to an ancient type of frog—an amphibian—than they are to lungfish. Clearly the missing link question has not yet been resolved.

What about another early coelacanth nickname the "living fossil" mentioned in 1939 newspaper headlines? Whether the coelacanth is truly a living fossil is a matter of perspective. While many fossil coelacanths have been found, none of them belong to the species *Latimeria chalumnae*. In that respect, *Latimeria chalumnae* isn't actually a living fossil.

Decades of research, however, have shown that *Latimeria chalumnae* has not radically evolved from the way coelacanths appeared millions of years ago. Its main body structure still very closely resembles that of ancient coelacanths. So studying *Latimeria chalumnae* is almost like being able to examine an ancient fossil as if it were alive. Modern coelacanth specimens have helped paleontologists confirm many theories based on ancient fossils.

Studying dead specimens of *Latimeria chalumnae* opened a door into the world of these fascinating fish. Researchers found many answers, but each one seemed to spark more questions. How do coelacanths swim? Do they live in groups? How do they hunt? And there was one nagging question from way back in 1939: do coelacanths walk on their lobed pectoral and pelvic fins, as J. L. B. Smith had thought? These questions could be answered only by watching live coelacanths.

CHAPTER FIVE

SUBMERSIBLE SEARCH

While French scientists studied coelacanths in the late 1950s, a young man in Germany was dreaming about the ancient fish. As a teenager, Hans Fricke read *Old Fourlegs*, J. L. B. Smith's book about the 1938 and 1952 discoveries. Fricke grew up to become a marine biologist. From time to time, he read articles about coelacanth research and expeditions that had tried and failed to capture a live specimen. Fricke longed to see a coelacanth himself. He even scuba dived along the coasts of Madagascar and the Comoro Islands, hoping to spot one.

SCIENTISTS CAN REMAIN DEEP UNDERWATER IN A SUBMERSIBLE LIKE *GEO* FOR MUCH LONGER PERIODS THAN THEY CAN WHILE SCUBA DIVING.

In 1987, Hans Fricke and a team of researchers from Germany's Max Planck Institute tried a new approach to the coelacanth quest. They designed and built a submersible—a miniature submarine—to dive deep in the water surrounding the Comoro Islands. The submersible, called *Geo*, was just large enough to carry two people to a depth of 700 feet (200 m). The team's goal was to find live coelacanths in their natural habitat.

At first, the team dove during the day. Safely inside *Geo,* they took turns cruising along the sandy ocean bottom and the nearby lava slopes, clifflike structures that were formed when ancient volcanoes erupted underwater. The team searched almost to the limit of *Geo's* range—waters where scientists believed the temperature was comfortable for coelacanths. But they saw nothing.

Next the searchers talked with several Comoran fishers, who told them they had caught coelacanths only at night. So the team tried night dives, but still they had no success. Hans Fricke was running out of time. He hated to leave the Comoro Islands, but he had important work waiting for him elsewhere. Jürgen Schauer, *Geo's* pilot, stayed on for a few more days.

DISCOVERY

On the evening of January 17, 1987, Jürgen Schauer piloted *Geo* to a depth of almost 700 feet (200 m). For half an hour Schauer and Olaf Reinicke, a student of Fricke's, cruised around the underwater rocks a short distance off the west coast of Grande Comore Island. *Geo's* spotlight shone into nooks and crannies. At nine o'clock, Schauer and Reinicke saw something move—something large and blue. "There it was, at the edge of the spotlight . . . I held my breath," Schauer recalled. As the fish moved, he saw its lobed fins. He had no doubt. It was a live coelacanth!

Schauer piloted *Geo* closer to the coelacanth. Unfortunately, his video camera failed, but a still camera worked. As the men took pictures, the coelacanth tipped forward, snout pointing downward, and did what looked like a headstand. The fish stayed in this odd position for more than a minute. Schauer found the movement graceful, but he had no idea why a coelacanth would move in this way.

Then *Geo* got too close. The coelacanth squeezed past the minisub, brushing against it, and swam quickly into darker water. One of its rough scales had broken off. Schauer picked it up with *Geo's* manipulator arm and brought it back to the surface. He already had photographs of the fish, but the scale was an unexpected bonus—and incontestable proof of their encounter.

A REMARKABLE SIGHT: A LIVE COELACANTH IN ITS NATURAL HABITAT

AN ACROBATIC COELACANTH DEMONSTRATES THE "HEADSTAND" THAT PUZZLED JÜRGEN SCHAUER AND THE FRICKE TEAM IN 1987.

40

The Fricke team returned to the same area during the next few nights and spotted more coelacanths. These successes ensured that the team's sponsors would provide funds for future dives. The researchers quickly planned a second expedition. That April, Fricke himself saw coelacanths at last. The team followed and filmed four of the fish, trailing one for six hours. As they observed the coelacanths, the researchers realized they could tell them apart by the white marks that dotted their bodies. These marks help the fish blend in with surrounding rocks, which are speckled with light-colored sponges and oysters. Every coelacanth has its own distinct pattern of white markings, so the researchers were able to track the movements of each one.

After the expedition, the Fricke team spent hours analyzing their videotapes of moving coelacanths. One unexpected discovery was that a coelacanth can move its lobed pectoral and pelvic fins similar to the way a person's arm swings through a shoulder socket. Even though a coelacanth's fins appear thick and awkward in comparison to other fishes' fins, they're actually quite flexible.

When a coelacanth swims, its pairs of lobed fins move the way a horse's legs do when it trots. The left pectoral fin moves

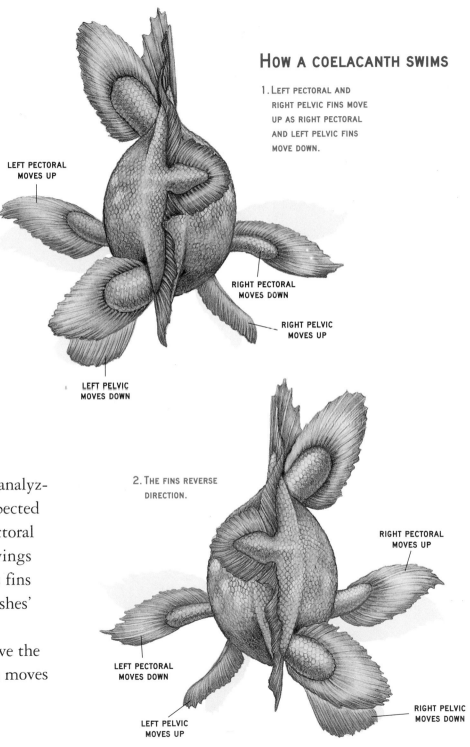

HOW A COELACANTH SWIMS

1. LEFT PECTORAL AND RIGHT PELVIC FINS MOVE UP AS RIGHT PECTORAL AND LEFT PELVIC FINS MOVE DOWN.

LEFT PECTORAL MOVES UP

RIGHT PECTORAL MOVES DOWN

RIGHT PELVIC MOVES UP

LEFT PELVIC MOVES DOWN

2. THE FINS REVERSE DIRECTION.

RIGHT PECTORAL MOVES UP

LEFT PECTORAL MOVES DOWN

LEFT PELVIC MOVES UP

RIGHT PELVIC MOVES DOWN

up at the same time as the right pelvic fin moves up. Then the fins reverse direction. A crawling child moves this way—the left arm moves forward as the right knee does. Lizards walk this way, too. Among fishes, this kind of intentional fin locomotion is unique to coelacanths.

Hans Fricke and his researchers also hoped to learn whether coelacanths walk on the ocean floor, as J. L. B. Smith had guessed. They observed that once in a while, a coelacanth rests close to the bottom. Its paired lobed fins might brush against or briefly rest on the bottom at those times. But the team never saw a coelacanth walk or stalk prey on its fins. Instead, it uses the fins to balance itself, to steer as it swims, and to brake when it needs to stop moving. It seemed that Smith's image of the fish as a crawling hunter had been mistaken.

Occasionally, the submersible startled a coelacanth. Then the fish needed a burst of speed. For quick getaways, a coelacanth uses its large, thick caudal fin. A few flips of this powerful fin work like the thrust of a rocket, propelling the coelacanth forward. Coelacanths don't seem to have enough energy to swim fast for a long time. They swim fast just long enough to escape danger; then they settle down.

Just as Jürgen Schauer had reported, the crew observed that many coelacanths did headstands when the submersible approached them. Other than the submersible, there didn't seem to be any threat or change in the water. Could the fish be responding to *Geo's* lights or its electromagnetic field?

To investigate, Fricke and his team fastened a pair of electrodes—metal posts that carry electricity—to *Geo's* manipulator arm. They passed a weak electrical current through the electrodes into the water. When they performed this test near two coelacanths, the fish did headstands! It appeared that the strange movement was indeed a response to the electrical current.

DIVING DEEPER

Collecting information during *Geo's* dives was exciting, but at times frustrating. The team could only watch from afar when a coelacanth swam into water deeper than 700 feet (200 m). *Geo* couldn't follow beyond this depth, so the team members decided to build a new submersible to expand their range.

Jürgen Schauer worked on *Jago* for the next two years. Named after a type of small, deep-sea shark, the submersible carries two people and can dive to a depth of 1,300 feet (400 m)—about twice as deep as *Geo*. *Jago* is 10.5 feet (3.2 m) long and 6.6 feet (2.0 m) wide. That may seem like a tight fit for two adult divers, but Karen Hissmann, a zoologist on the Fricke team, says that "this is enough space to lay down and stretch. [We don't] feel imprisoned because there are two large windows."

Jago was designed to be a diving laboratory. Temperature probes, cameras, sonar equipment, and a manipulator arm allow the scientists on board to collect a wealth of information about creatures and the surrounding environment. And according to Hissmann, "Diving with a research submersible like *Jago* is much, much less dangerous than driving a car. We have regular technical and safety checks. [We built] *Jago* ourselves . . . so whenever Jürgen gets the impression that [anything] could be changed or improved, he does it."

By the end of 1989, the Fricke team was back in the Comoro Islands with their new submersible and ready to track down more coelacanths. Thinking the fish spent their days in water close to 1,300 feet (400 m) deep, the team piloted *Jago* past the shallow slopes and headed straight toward the bottom. While they saw many interesting fishes and plants on the way down, they didn't find any coelacanths. Neither the smooth slopes of deeper waters nor the sandy ocean floor had hiding places for large fish, so perhaps this area wasn't a suitable habitat for coelacanths.

The team decided to return the search to shallower water and explore the caves that pit the rocky slopes at about 700 feet (200 m) deep. A cave seemed like a strange place for such a large fish to lurk, but they had looked everywhere else. Much to their surprise, when they shone their spotlight into a cave, circles of light gleamed back at them. They were the eyes of resting coelacanths.

The *Jago* crew eventually found coelacanths living in twenty caves along the coasts of Grande Comore Island and Anjouan Island. The caves ranged in depth from 538 to 797 feet (164–243 m) below the water's surface, and they extended 6.5 to 9.5 feet (2.0–3.0 m) into the rock. Although the team hadn't expected to find coelacanths in caves, they realized that these hiding places provide protection from strong water currents as the fish rest during the day. The caves' rough walls and jutting overhangs also discourage predators from entering.

In their caves, coelacanths stay almost motionless for hours at a time. Scientists believe this is a strategy to save energy. The bodies of some animals change food into energy quickly. But a coelacanth's body changes food into energy very slowly. Keeping still helps a coelacanth conserve the energy it has.

Small groups of up to ten coelacanths often occupy the same cave. The Fricke team observed that the coelacanths showed no aggression toward one another. Do the fish recognize other individuals? The team never saw any signs of communication among them.

HANS FRICKE (LEFT) AND JÜRGEN SCHAUER INSIDE *JAGO*

On the rare occasions when a coelacanth's fin brushed against another's body, the contact was brief, faster than the blink of an eye.

Jago has helped the team investigate the coelacanth's habit of doing headstands. Reflecting on their many expeditions, the researchers realized that while the fish had often responded to *Geo's* presence by doing headstands, they seldom did them when *Jago* approached. Only when the newer submersible got very close did the headstands begin. *Jago* has a lower electromagnetic field than *Geo.* Perhaps, the team theorizes, it bothers the fish less. According to Karen Hissmann, "This curious [headstand] behavior is still a mystery. We speculate this posture has something to do with the function of the rostral organ." The answer awaits future research.

Observations from *Jago* and *Geo* have also helped the Fricke team begin to solve another coelacanth mystery—the purpose of the epicaudal fin. Knowing that this "extra" tail fin is unique among modern fishes, scientists had wondered for decades how it's used. The submersible divers learned that it can bend separately from the large caudal fin. A coelacanth beats and bends the epicaudal fin to maneuver into a headstand and to steer around obstacles. The fish may be aided in these movements by sensory cells that extend to the tip of the fin. These cells probably help coelacanths detect water currents and determine which way to bend the epicaudal fin.

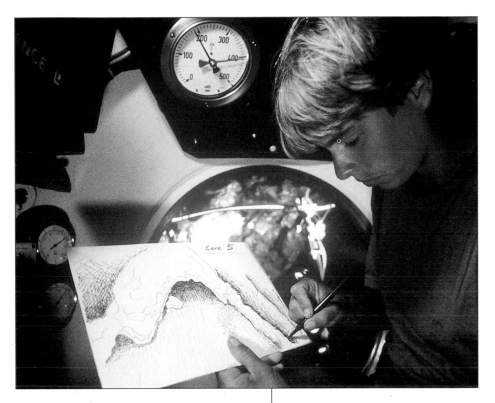

KAREN HISSMANN PAINSTAKINGLY MAPS A COELACANTH CAVE FROM INSIDE *JAGO.*

FISH TRACKERS

Hans Fricke and his colleagues knew that coelacanths moved around at night, probably to hunt. After all, it was then that fishers caught them and that Jürgen Schauer had first seen one. The fishes that coelacanths eat are active at night, too. But where do coelacanths go during their nightly swims?

Following the fish in *Jago* wasn't the way to find out. Coelacanths didn't seem to engage in normal swimming behavior when the submersible came near. Fricke and Schauer decided to try attaching sound transmitters to a few coelacanths. These devices send out sound signals as the tagged animal moves. Instruments far from the animal receive the signals. Then scientists can pinpoint the animal's location and track its movements.

Tagging a coelacanth posed a problem for the Fricke team. The usual way to tag a fish was to shoot a small dart into its body. To do that, a team member would have to swim outside of *Jago.* At such great depths, the huge pressure of the water would harm the diver. It wouldn't work to bring a coelacanth to the surface and tag it there, either—that would probably kill the fish.

The team solved the problem by inventing a new way to tag fish in deep water. They designed a special air gun and mounted it in *Jago's* hull. From inside *Jago,* the team shot darts into the scales of eleven coelacanths. Attached to each dart was a sound transmitter tag. Designed to fall off on their own after several weeks, the darts and tags did not harm or disturb the fish.

After *Jago* left the scene, the coelacanths went about their normal routine. The transmitters sent sound signals to a boat on the surface, so the team could track the movements of each fish. They learned that at dusk, the coelacanths slowly swam away from their caves to hunt. Many other fishes move upward at night to hunt in shallower water, where prey is more abundant. But the coelacanths observed by the team traveled downward, into deeper water.

Why would coelacanths go deep to hunt? Fricke and his team have two ideas. First, more fishes that coelacanths eat—such as cardinal fish and deep-water snappers—live in deep water than in shallow water. Second, deep water is cooler than shallow water. A coelacanth's small gills can absorb more oxygen from cooler water than from warmer water. A hunting coelacanth probably needs the extra oxygen and the energy boost it gives.

In addition to tracking coelacanths with transmitters, the *Jago* team members watched coelacanths hunt from the submersible as much as the fish would allow. They learned that a coelacanth hunts alone by drifting along with the water current. As the coelacanth's body drifts, it uses its fins to steer. By letting water currents move its body instead of swimming strenuously, a coelacanth saves energy that it needs to catch its prey. (This type of hunting, called drift hunting, is also characteristic of some other deep-sea fishes.) After its night of hunting, a coelacanth heads to the nearest cave. It may not be the one it used the previous day. By sunrise, the fish is again resting quietly.

A SOUND TRANSMITTER IS VISIBLE BETWEEN THIS COELACANTH'S REAR DORSAL FIN AND CAUDAL FIN.

PROTECTING THE COELACANTH

As Hans Fricke and his colleagues learned more about coelacanths, they became concerned about the future of these fascinating fish. The team's counts of the population suggested that fishing was taking a significant toll. What had once seemed like an important means of obtaining specimens for study now appeared to be threatening the very animal scientists wanted to learn so much about.

The Fricke team and coelacanth experts from South Africa began to educate people about the importance of protecting coelacanths. Thanks in part to their efforts, in 1989 coelacanths were declared endangered by the Convention on International Trade in Endangered Species (CITES). This international agreement controls the trade of threatened and endangered species. When the Comoro Islands signed the agreement in 1994, the legal coelacanth trade ended. If a coelacanth is caught accidentally, it can be sent only to a scientist or museum, and then only if CITES grants permission.

The Comoran people are also making a difference. Concerned Comorans worked with local fishers to gain their support for a marine park where the fish would have some protection. These efforts led to the establishment of a park on the southwest coast of Grande Comore.

The number of coelacanths caught each year seems to be going down, probably because fewer people fish at night and because the deep-fishing methods that resulted in accidental catches of coelacanths aren't used as often as they

COMORAN CHILDREN EXAMINE A DEAD COELACANTH CAPTURED BY FISHERS. A LONG POLE WAS INSERTED THROUGH THE FISH'S MOUTH AFTER IT DIED SO THAT THE FISHERS COULD TRANSPORT IT.

were in the past. When the Fricke team returned to the islands in November 2000, they were encouraged to find that the coelacanth population in their main observation area had not declined since their last count. Karen Hissmann reported, "We encountered many of our old friends, which is always a delight. Some of them we [have] known now for more than ten years, and they still look the same."

The Fricke team and other scientists still have many coelacanth puzzles to solve, such as how the fish find and capture their food in inky black water. Since it's too dark to see, does a coelacanth use its rostral organ to sense prey, as some scientists suspect? And what about Keith Thomson's theory about the head joint in the skull? Does it create suction that helps a hunting coelacanth suck in prey?

The Fricke team's dives in *Geo* and *Jago* have given the world an exciting glimpse into the world of living coelacanths. What's it like to be part of a team that makes scientific history with almost every expedition? For Karen Hissmann, "Every dive in *Jago* is extremely exciting. [We] always enter a space and area which are mostly unknown. We do not know what we will see. Usually we encounter organisms which [have never been] seen and filmed in their natural habitat before. It is a kind of pioneer feeling."

THESE COMORAN STAMPS HAVE HELPED PROMOTE AWARENESS OF THE NEED TO PROTECT COELACANTHS.

CHAPTER SIX

KING OF THE SEA

The next chapter in the coelacanth story began not in the Comoro Islands, but 6,000 miles (10,000 km) away, in Sulawesi, Indonesia. Mark Erdmann, an American marine biologist, works and lives in this Asian nation. On September 18, 1997, he and his wife, Arnaz Mehta Erdmann, went on a house-hunting expedition with two friends. The group stopped at a fish market in the city of Manado. There Arnaz noticed a man wheeling a large cart across the parking lot. What caught her attention the most was the four-foot-long fish inside it. She called to Mark and the others to come take a look at the curious creature.

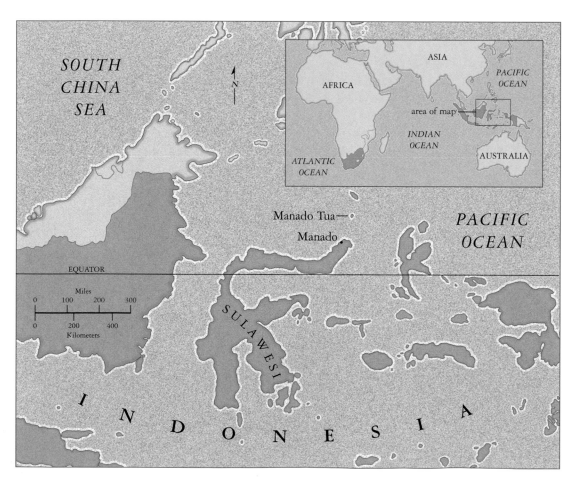

Mark Erdmann easily recognized the fish as a coelacanth—like Hans Fricke, he had read *Old Fourlegs* as a boy. He knew that coelacanths lived around the Comoro Islands. Earlier in the 1990s at least three had been caught short distances from the islands—one near Mozambique and two near Madagascar. Erdmann had never heard that the fish lived in Indonesia too. Since no one else in the market appeared excited or even interested, he figured others had already seen and reported coelacanths from this area. Still, he knew a good fish story when he saw one. He thought about buying the coelacanth, but a fish more than four feet long is difficult to store in a small hotel room. Instead, he borrowed a camera from his friend and took three pictures.

While Mark took the pictures, Arnaz asked the fisher where he had caught the coelacanth. He told her it came from the deep water around Manado Tua, a volcanic island not far off the northern coast of Sulawesi. He had seen others like it in the past, but rarely. "If this did turn out to be a major discovery," the Erdmanns decided, "we could always find another fish during [Mark's] two-year project in Manado."

A short time later, Mark Erdmann flew to the United States and visited his research adviser at the University of California-Berkeley, marine biology professor Roy Caldwell. Erdmann was shocked to learn that no one had ever reported seeing a coelacanth in Indonesia. He had stumbled onto an incredible find!

Like J. L. B. Smith, Eric Hunt, and many others, Mark Erdmann caught coelacanth fever. Back in Indonesia, he and Arnaz interviewed fishers and showed them photographs of coelacanths, just as J. L. B. and Margaret Smith had. Within six months, they identified a group of fishers who fished for sharks and deep-water snappers. The nets they used extended deeper than 1,000 feet (300 m) in the water—definitely coelacanth territory.

WHEN MARK ERDMANN PHOTOGRAPHED THIS COELACANTH IN AN INDONESIAN FISH MARKET, HE HAD NO IDEA THAT SCIENTISTS HAD NEVER RECORDED SUCH A SIGHTING IN THE AREA.

OM LAMEK SONATHAM (CENTER) AND HIS CREW PROUDLY DISPLAY A CATCH THAT WOULD SOON MAKE SCIENTIFIC HISTORY.

The fishers spoke of a creature they called *raja laut*, or "king of the sea," whose description matched the coelacanth. Om Lamek Sonatham, a fisher from Manado Tua, told Mark that he caught a *raja laut* two or three times a year. Mark told the fishers he wanted a specimen and gave them his address. Then—again like J. L. B. Smith—he waited.

A RAJA LAUT FOR SCIENCE

The morning of July 30, 1998, a boat stopped at the beach in front of the Erdmanns' house near Manado. One of the people on board was Om Lamek Sonatham. His son, Samuel, stepped out of the boat into shallow water to greet the Erdmanns. He had a huge smile on his face and a huge fish in his arms. It was a coelacanth—and it was still alive!

Cameras in hand, the Erdmanns raced across the sand. The coelacanth, which Om Lamek Sonatham had netted during the night, floated in the shallow water. Several of its scales were missing, and it was bleeding slightly. The Erdmanns realized the fish was close to death. While Mark snapped photographs, Arnaz shot video film of the coelacanth as it swam slowly. It kept turning belly up, a position fish often assume shortly before they die.

The Erdmanns attached a rope to the coelacanth and used a boat to pull it through the water. They hoped the steady flow of water over the fish's gills would revive it. For a short time, the fish seemed better. The Erdmanns got into the water and swam alongside it for more than an hour. In the bright daylight, the coelacanth's eyes shone with a greenish glow. Its scales caught the sunlight and reflected back tiny golden flashes.

Were the Erdmanns afraid of the coelacanth? "Fear was the last emotion that either of us had," Mark recalled. "Wonder, awe, and a feeling of being very lucky to be able to swim with this fish were the more dominant emotions. This animal, at least, was much more gentle and slow-moving than ferocious, and its totally calm manner left no doubt that it would be safe [for us] to swim with it." In fact, Mark's major worry was that a shark would attack the weakened fish.

No sharks attacked, but unfortunately, the coelacanth's strength failed again. This time the Erdmanns could do nothing more to save it. During the 1990s, scientists had discovered more about the reasons captured coelacanths die. The problem isn't sunlight, water temperature, or the quick trip up from deep water.

The fish die for two reasons. First, struggling against a fishhook or net uses up a lot of energy and oxygen. A struggling coelacanth needs extra oxygen, but its small gills can't absorb much oxygen quickly. Without enough oxygen, the fish slowly suffocates.

Second, during a hard struggle a coelacanth's body produces a waste product called lactic acid, which pours into the fish's muscles. (Other animals, including humans, also produce lactic acid during exertion.) Too much lactic acid

causes a complex combination of physiological and chemical problems. Unable to process the overload, certain body systems fail. Together, the lack of oxygen and the excess of lactic acid cause a great deal of stress—enough to kill the fish.

Unable to save the coelacanth's life, the Erdmanns knew that saving its body was crucial. It was absolute proof that coelacanths lived in Indonesia. With the fish on board, they raced in a speedboat to Manado, where quick freezing of the body safely preserved the fish for future study.

In September 1998, Mark wrote a short article about his find for *Nature*. Once again, coelacanths hit the headlines. Reporters and other interested people swarmed into Manado to question the Erdmanns and local fishers. Would the coelacanth population be plundered by scientists and collectors in search of specimens? Mark began work to publicize the importance of protecting the fish. The Indonesian Institute of Sciences helped out with a media campaign. Fortunately, the Indonesian government soon passed a law proclaiming the coelacanth a national treasure. As such it is strictly protected from being captured or traded.

Since the law's passage, Indonesians have joined in the efforts to protect their coelacanths. Children have enthusiastically participated in a drawing contest and other activities that focus on saving the fish. People who live near the fish's home waters make and sell coelacanth handicrafts, such as carved hair clips, necklaces, and napkin rings. In this way, such artisans earn a living without harming coelacanths. And local pride in the Indonesian coelacanth as a national treasure has influenced fishers to turn away

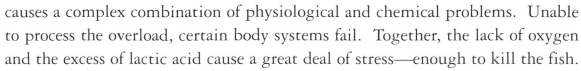

AN INDONESIAN ARTISAN CARVES A COELACANTH HANDICRAFT.

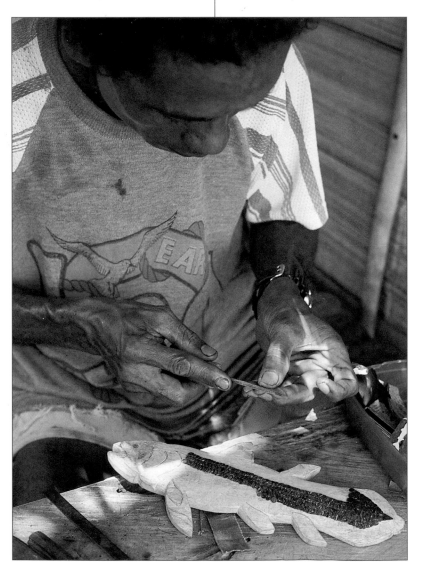

aquarium collectors who wish to illegally capture live specimens for display.

Mark Erdmann's next job was to determine if the Indonesian coelacanth was a *Latimeria chalumnae,* the same species as the Comoran coelacanth. It looked very much like one—it had whitish spots, similar fins, and six rostral openings. The only difference seemed to be the color. The Indonesian specimen was brownish-gray, not the steel-blue color seen in the Comoro Islands. The golden glints of the Indonesian coelacanth's scales had never been seen on a Comoran catch either. Was it possible the Indonesian coelacanths were a new species?

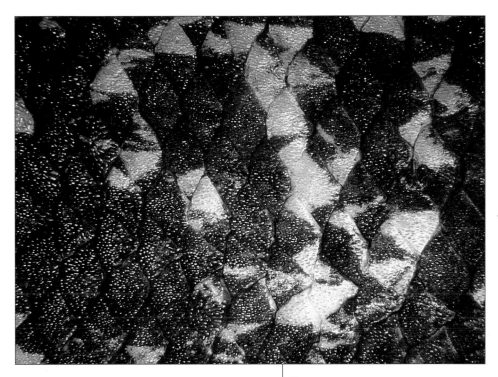

THE GOLD-FLECKED SCALES OF ERDMANN'S SPECIMEN SEEMED TO SET IT APART FROM *LATIMERIA CHALUMNAE.*

Erdmann and the scientists he worked with at the Indonesian Institute of Sciences arranged to test the specimen's DNA to find out. Found in the cells of all living things, DNA carries the pattern of characteristics that pass from a parent to its offspring. Some of these characteristics, like eye color and hair color in humans, are individual. Others, like organs and their functions, are specific to a given species. The results of the tests seemed to indicate a new species, but Erdmann put off making an announcement. He wanted his group to make an accurate comparison between the shape and measurements of the Indonesian coelacanth and those of Comoran coelacanths. After this careful study, he would feel confident in claiming that his specimen was a new species.

While Erdmann and his colleagues worked, they heard some very upsetting news. A French scientist named Laurent Pouyaud and five Indonesian coauthors had published an article about a "new species" of coelacanth—Erdmann's coelacanth—in a French scientific journal! Pouyaud had obtained a tissue sample of Erdmann's fish from the Indonesian Institute of Sciences. He quickly published his own test results.

Since Pouyaud's article contained the first full description that determined the fish was a new species, he chose its name. Indonesian and Comoran coelacanths belong to the same genus, so he had to use the genus name *Latimeria*. He chose *Latimeria menadoensis* as the species name, after the area of Indonesia where Om Lamek Sonatham had caught the coelacanth.

Laurent Pouyaud's actions angered scientists from many countries. To them, Mark Erdmann and his colleagues had been robbed of credit for work they had rightfully done. Erdmann called Pouyaud's action a "shameless act of scientific piracy." He was especially disappointed because he hadn't intended to publish the DNA test results himself. He believed that honor, and the honor of naming the fish, belonged to his Indonesian colleagues.

Shortly after the appearance of Pouyaud's article, Erdmann and other scientists published a paper that refuted some of Pouyaud's results and supplied a more detailed DNA analysis of the Indonesian fish. The importance of the discovery of *Latimeria menadoensis,* as well as many scientists' desire to learn more about it, gradually eclipsed the debate.

LATIMERIA MENADOENSIS, AS NAMED BY LAURENT POUYAUD. THE SPECIMEN WEIGHED 64 POUNDS (29 KG) AND MEASURED 4.1 FEET (1.2 M).

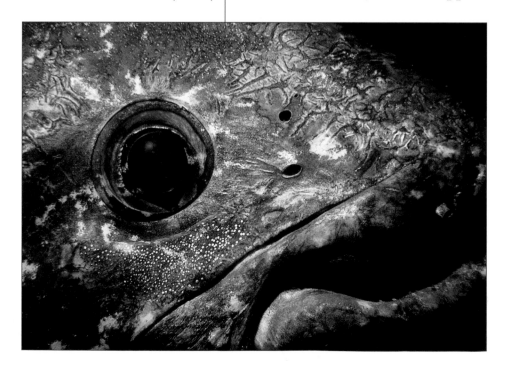

JAGO JOINS THE SEARCH

Among the many people excited to learn about the Indonesian coelacanth were Hans Fricke and his research team. Toward the end of 1999, the Fricke team brought *Jago* to Indonesia to look for the fish. They conducted seven dives near Manado Tua, but found no coelacanths in the areas they searched.

A few days before the expedition's end, Karen Hissmann and Jürgen Schauer dove off the coast of Sulawesi, 225 miles (362 km) southwest of Manado Tua. Unlike the lava slopes around the Comoro Islands and Manado Tua, the slopes in this area are made of a kind of rock called calcium carbonate. Since Comoran coelacanths live only near lava slopes, Hissmann and Schauer weren't really expecting to find any coelacanths there. Imagine their surprise when they peeked into a deep cave and found two!

Unfortunately, the expedition's time limit ran out just as Hissmann and Schauer made this discovery, so the team couldn't investigate further at that time. Scientists still don't know how large the population of Indonesian coelacanths is or exactly where they live, but local fishers claim to have caught many coelacanths near Manado Tua. Perhaps future expeditions will discover more about Indonesia's "king of the sea" and its home.

Chapter Seven

BACK TO SOUTH AFRICA

October 28, 2000, looked like a great day for scuba diving in Sodwana Bay, South Africa. Pieter Venter, Peter Timm, and Etienne le Roux donned their scuba gear and slipped into the water. Venter was hoping this dive would qualify him for certification as a Trimix diver. This type of deep-water diving is particularly dangerous and requires the use of three gases—oxygen, nitrogen, and helium—to keep divers safe.

Pieter Venter swam into Jesser Canyon and descended to a depth of 342 feet (104 m). As he paddled slowly along the rocky ledges, he saw something gleam.

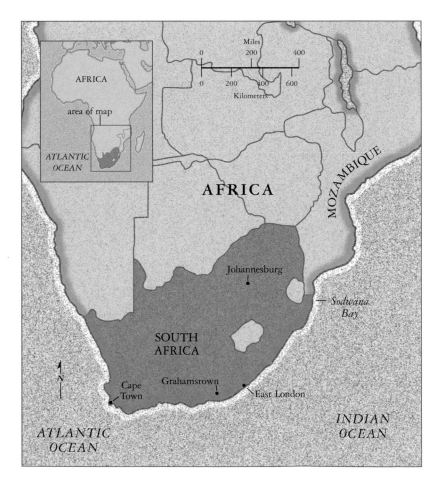

"I saw this eye reflecting towards me and that made me curious," Venter recalled. "I approached . . . and underneath an overhang, I saw a fish of about 2 meters [6 feet] long. I looked at it carefully and after about six seconds I suddenly realized it was a coelacanth."

Venter signaled to Peter Timm, who swam over and joined him. Together they searched farther along the rocky ledges and saw two more coelacanths. Venter's amazement quickly turned to frustration. He didn't have a camera with him, so he had no way to prove what he had seen. "It was like seeing a UFO without taking a photograph."

To many ichthyologists, comparing those coelacanths to something as remarkable as a UFO would seem perfectly logical. Coelacanths had never before been found swimming freely in water shallower than about 490 feet (150 m). And a person had never before swum near a coelacanth in its natural habitat.

Without proof of their discovery, the divers decided not to announce it yet. Instead, they formed a group with several other divers and returned in November 2000. This time they brought two cameramen—and their determination to find more coelacanths and film them.

On November 27, the team was ready to go. The dive was scheduled to last 134 minutes—more than two hours—but most of that time had to be used to travel back up to the surface. Deep-water divers must ascend very slowly to protect themselves from a condition known as decompression sickness.

People who venture into deep water enter an environment of extreme pressure due to the weight of the water around them. This pressure compresses the air a diver breathes. When air is compressed, its molecules are pushed closer together, so a given amount of air takes up less space when compressed than when uncompressed. A diver who breathes compressed air inhales more air with each breath than the body normally processes.

One component of air, nitrogen, can't be processed by the body at all. On the surface, humans exhale nitrogen with every breath. In deep water, a diver does the same thing. But because the diver is inhaling extra nitrogen in the form of compressed air, the lungs take longer than usual to exhale all of it.

As a diver ascends to the surface, the pressure drops, allowing the nitrogen molecules to expand in the diver's body. If the diver doesn't exhale this nitrogen promptly, it forms bubbles in the blood. Nitrogen bubbles can prevent blood from flowing, causing decompression sickness. The results can include pain, injury, and sometimes death. To prevent decompression sickness, divers pause periodically during an ascent to allow the body to rid itself of the extra nitrogen.

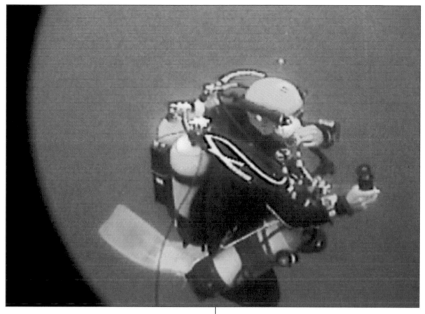

PIETER VENTER EXPLORES JESSER CANYON. THIS PHOTOGRAPH WAS TAKEN FROM THE TEAM'S UNDERWATER VIDEOTAPE.

Because of the long time needed to ascend, the divers would have only fifteen minutes of bottom time for exploring at the lowest depth. Could they find a coelacanth in such a short time?

After descending, the divers swam along the rocks and searched the deep, craggy overhangs and stony ledges at a depth of 344 feet (105 m). Time was running out. Then, twelve minutes into the bottom time, the divers spotted three coelacanths! The fish ranged in length from 3 to 6 feet (1–2 m). All three were swimming with their heads pointing downward toward the ledge.

Christo Serfontein and Dennis Harding, the two cameramen, got busy. They shot video footage of the fish and took still photographs. Too soon, the bottom time ran out—but the team had found what they sought. Elated, they began their ascent. Then something terrible happened. A problem with his air supply caused Christo Serfontein to lose consciousness. Dennis Harding helped him to the surface as quickly as he could—too quickly. When the men reached the boat, Harding complained of neck pains. It was clear that both were in terrible danger.

There are two ways to stop decompression sickness after a diver ascends too rapidly. If the diver can immediately drop back down toward deeper water—and greater pressure—a very slow, carefully timed ascent can prevent nitrogen bubbles from forming in the blood. A diver can also enter a decompression chamber, a room where pressure like that of deep water can be created to protect the diver from illness.

Unfortunately, Dennis Harding collapsed and died before either of these remedies could be attempted. Christo Serfontein was taken back underwater and later treated in a decompression chamber, after which he recovered. The disastrous accident and the loss of Harding's life saddened everyone on the expedition. It was a terrible reminder that underwater exploration is dangerous even for experienced divers.

In spite of the risk, Venter and his Trimix team were eager to learn more about the Sodwana Bay coelacanths. In May 2001, the group began a new series of dives. In one spot, at a depth of 338 feet (103 m), the divers discovered a coelacanth they had never seen before. Intriguingly, this coelacanth wasn't in Jesser Canyon, where the previous fish had been spotted. The unexpected find indicated that the population of South African coelacanths may be more widespread than the team had thought.

On the last day of the expedition, while diving in Jesser Canyon, the team spotted two coelacanths. Venter recognized one as a fish the team had seen the previous November, but he immediately knew the other coelacanth was a new one. It was huge—at least 6.5 feet (2.0 m) long. According to coelacanth specialist Robin Stobbs, this fish is "the largest living coelacanth ever seen or recorded to date." Venter's team had made coelacanth history again.

WHAT'S NEXT?

For decades, South African coelacanth specialists had believed that coelacanths lurk in the underwater canyons, caves, and overhangs that dot the South African coast, not just near the Comoro Islands, Madagascar, Mozambique, and Sulawesi. The sightings in 2000 and 2001 confirmed their belief and raised new questions. Are the Sodwana Bay fish a separate coelacanth species? How many of these fish are there? Why do they live in shallower water than their counterparts in the Comoro Islands and Indonesia? Could the 1939 coelacanth have been part of this population?

One thing that seems to be certain is that the South African coelacanths discovered by Pieter Venter are safe from too much interference by humans. They live in a sanctuary, a place where it's against the law to disturb or harm any animals. No one can dive there without permission from the South African government, and no one can harm a coelacanth for any reason.

In the future, scientists hope to explore the area's large underwater canyons and perhaps place a video camera underwater. Another promising tool is a small, unmanned vehicle called a Remotely Operated Vehicle (ROV). Operated from a boat on the surface, an ROV could wind around overhangs and into spaces too narrow for manned submersibles like *Jago*. Cameras inside the ROV could film the slopes. Plans are underway for manned submersible dives as well.

While some coelacanth puzzles have been solved, many still remain. In 2001, a fourth coelacanth was caught off the coast of Madagascar. Does a significant population may live in that area? Later that year, a coelacanth was caught near Kenya—another first. Do other undiscovered groups of coelacanths live elsewhere?

One certain topic of future investigation concerns the world's youngest coelacanths. Where do pups live and grow? "This is the million dollar question!" says Robin Stobbs. So far, no one has found live pups in their natural habitat. They don't seem to live in the caves where adults spend their days. (Living away from adults might be a smart strategy for a coelacanth pup, since it's about the size of an adult's prey.)

Some scientists believe pups live in very deep water, below 2,000 feet (600 m). At this depth, however,

REMOTELY OPERATED VEHICLES LIKE THIS ONE MAY BE CRUCIAL TO THE FUTURE OF COELACANTH STUDIES.

prey may be scarce—and most growing fish eat a lot. In the Comoro Islands, hiding from predators at this depth would also be difficult, since there are fewer caves and crevices in such deep water.

Other scientists believe pups live in shallower water than adults. The wealth of fish found in warm, shallow water would meet a pup's food needs, and small caves and crevices in the rocky slopes would provide thousands of hiding places. Fishers from the Comoros, Madagascar, and Sulawesi say they have caught pups in shallow water. Even though the fishers may be informed and reliable, their reports can't be accepted as scientific evidence. A photograph or a specimen is needed as proof.

THE DISCOVERY OF LIVE PUPS WOULD REVEAL IMPORTANT NEW INFORMATION ABOUT HOW COELACANTHS LIVE. THIS UNBORN 14-INCH (34-CM) PUP WAS TAKEN FROM THE BODY OF A FEMALE CAUGHT NEAR MOZAMBIQUE.

While scientists disagree on where pups live, they all agree that they must be found. "We *have* to discover where the pups are born and where they spend their early years," says Stobbs. Pups could be captured, tagged with identifying markers, and released. Later, the tagged pups could be recaptured and measured to reveal how fast coelacanths grow. The whole life story of the coelacanth can't be told until the pup puzzle has been solved.

Scientists agree that the only way they will fully understand coelacanths is by studying captive specimens. But the groups of coelacanths found so far contain few individuals, so it wouldn't be wise to remove any for captive study. These fish are the adults that will produce new pups and keep the species alive. Besides, no one has figured out how to keep an adult coelacanth alive once it's been brought to the surface.

Pups, however, might be good candidates for captive study. Young animals are usually more adaptable to new surroundings than adults, so pups might survive transport to the surface. But some people argue that capturing even a few pups could cause great harm to the coelacanth population. They insist that captive study of coelacanths shouldn't even be considered until scientists are sure that the fish aren't endangered.

The question of who would keep a captured coelacanth is also controversial. Judging by the crowds that flocked to see Marjorie Courtenay-Latimer's specimen and the public fervor generated by the Erdmanns' discovery, a live coelacanth would become an instant tourist attraction—a moneymaker and an object of prestige for the nation that owned it. Would nations compete with each other to bring home a live coelacanth, further depleting the population? The scientists who attended a coelacanth conference in 2000 agreed that any captured fish should remain in the country where the capture occurred. Agreements like this one may help avoid future conflicts.

Although the modern coelacanth species make the headlines more often, coelacanth fossils still pose intriguing questions. For one hundred years, scientists believed coelacanths were extinct because the most recent fossils ever found were seventy million years old. Where are the fossils of the coelacanths that have lived since then? Scientists think they must exist somewhere. Perhaps they're buried deep in a place where humans can't dig, such as beneath the ocean floor. If any are ever found, they may provide clues to how ancient coelacanths survived through the ages.

While it's usually people that catch coelacanths, something about coelacanths also "catches" people. As future scientists solve today's coelacanth mysteries, they may discover others. Someone new will catch coelacanth fever. And when that happens, another exciting quest is sure to follow.

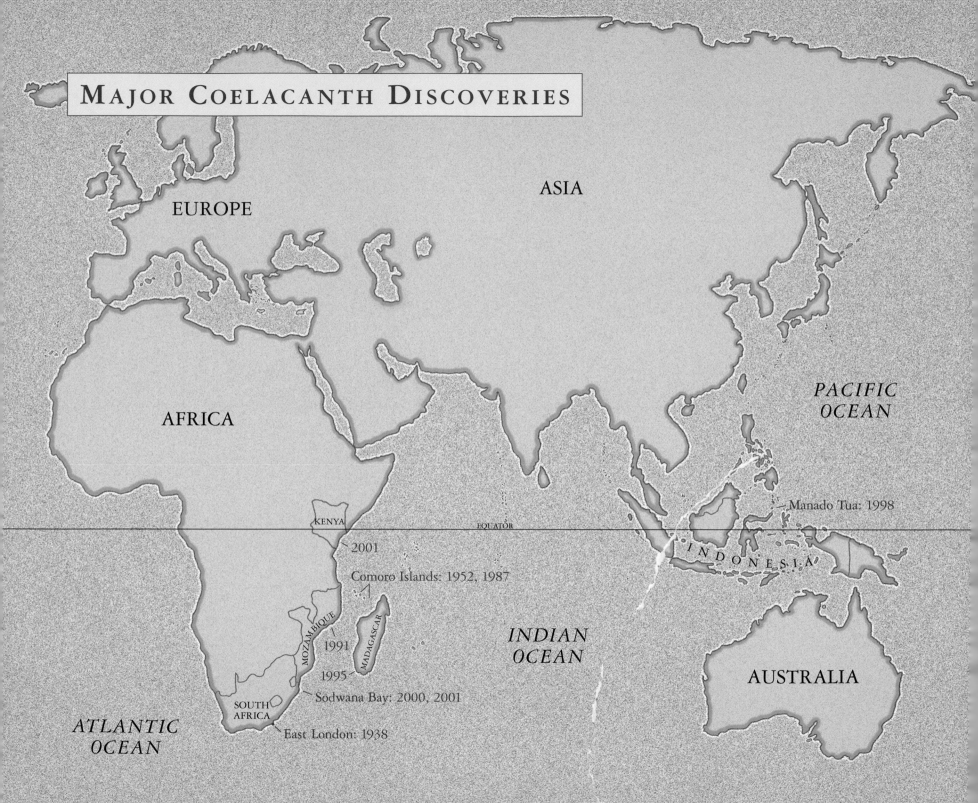

Major Coelacanth Discoveries

EUROPE

ASIA

AFRICA

PACIFIC
OCEAN

Manado Tua: 1998

KENYA

EQUATOR

2001

Comoro Islands: 1952, 1987

INDONESIA

MOZAMBIQUE

MADAGASCAR

INDIAN
OCEAN

1991

AUSTRALIA

1995

Sodwana Bay: 2000, 2001

SOUTH
AFRICA

ATLANTIC
OCEAN

East London: 1938

TIMELINE

1938	Museum curator Marjorie Courtenay-Latimer salvages a mysterious fish from a fishing boat in East London, South Africa.
1939	Ichthyologist J. L. B. Smith identifies the fish as a coelacanth and names it *Latimeria chalumnae.*
1952	Comoran fisher Ahamadi Abdallah captures a coelacanth off the island of Anjouan.
1953	Jacques Millot leads French scientists in studying a third coelacanth.
1955	Millot and his colleagues discover eggs in the body of a female coelacanth.
1956	Smith publishes *Old Fourlegs: The Story of the Coelacanth.*
1966	Keith Thomson discovers the coelacanth's unique head joint.
1975	Scientists discover unborn pups inside a female coelacanth, proving that coelacanths are ovoviviparous.
1987	Jürgen Schauer and Olaf Reinicke, members of Hans Fricke's *Geo* submersible team, see a live coelacanth in its natural habitat.
1989	The Fricke team uses a new submersible, *Jago,* to locate coelacanths living in caves.
1991	A Japanese fishing boat catches a female coelacanth off the coast of Mozambique.
1995	Fishers net a coelacanth near Madagascar.
1997	Mark Erdmann identifies a coelacanth in an Indonesian fish market.
1998	Indonesian fisher Om Lamek Sonatham catches a coelacanth near Manado Tua and delivers it to Mark Erdmann.
1999	Erdmann's specimen is determined to be a new species. French scientist Laurent Pouyaud publishes a description ahead of Erdmann's team, naming the fish *Latimeria menadoensis.*
2000	Pieter Venter and his diving team discover and film coelacanths in Sodwana Bay, South Africa—the first time scuba divers have seen coelacanths. One diver loses his life in the expedition.
2001	Venter's team discovers the largest coelacanth yet, a specimen at least 6.5 feet (2.0 m) long. Later that year, the first coelacanth catch off the coast of Kenya is confirmed.

Source Notes

Page 6   Marjorie Courtenay-Latimer, "Reminiscences of the Discovery of the Coelacanth, *Latimeria Chalumnae* Smith," *Cryptozoology* 8 (1988): 4.

6   Marjorie Courtenay-Latimer, letter to author, September 27, 2000.

6–7   Courtenay-Latimer, "Reminiscences," 4.

8   Ibid., 6.

12   Ibid., 9.

13   Samantha Weinberg, *A Fish Caught in Time: The Search for the Coelacanth* (New York: HarperCollins, 2000), 30.

13   Ibid.

13   Ibid.

13   J. L. B. Smith, *Old Fourlegs: The Story of the Coelacanth* (London: Longmans, Green and Co., 1956), 50.

14   Ibid.

16   Ibid., 60.

22   Ibid., 85.

22   Ibid., 105.

23   Ibid., 109.

25   Ibid., 143.

25   Ibid., 145.

26   Ibid., 146.

Page 39   Weinberg, 138.

39   Ibid.

43   Karen Hissmann, e-mail to author, October 13, 2000.

43   Ibid.

45   Karen Hissmann, e-mail to author, February 12, 2001.

49   Karen Hissmann, e-mail to author, October 13, 2000.

49   Ibid.

51   Mark Erdmann, "A New Home for 'Old Fourlegs,'" *California Wild*, July 13, 2001, <http://www.calacademy.org/publications/calwild/spring2000/html/fourlegs.html>, spring 2000.

53   Erdmann, e-mail to author, November 22, 2000.

53   [photo caption] Weinberg, 179.

56   Ibid.

58   Reuters, "'Living Fossils' Discovered Off South African Coast," CNN.com, July 13, 2001, <http://www.cnn.com/2000/NATURE/12/01/living.fossils.reut/>, Dec. 1, 2000.

58   Ibid.

61   Robin Stobbs, e-mail to author, May 24, 2001.

62   Stobbs, e-mail to author, November 11, 2000.

63   Ibid.

Photo Acknowledgments

The publisher gratefully acknowledges the use of photographs from the following sources: © Mark Erdmann, front cover, pp. 51, 52, 53, 54, 55, 56, 65; © Ian Cartwright/PhotoDisc, back cover; The Natural History Museum, London, pp. 1, 11, 36; J. L. B. Smith Institute of Ichthyology, p. 9 (both); Robin Stobbs, pp. 12, 18, 20, 21, 24, 26, 33, 35, 63; © Bettmann/CORBIS, pp. 27, 28; © AP/Wide World Photos, p. 30; © Hans Fricke, MPIV Seewiesen, p. 38; © Jürgen Schauer/Hans Fricke, MPIV Seewiesen, pp. 39, 40 (all), 42, 47; © L. Kasung/JAGO-Team, MPIV Seewiesen, p. 44; © Jürgen Schauer/JAGO-Team, MPIV Seewiesen, p. 45; © Karen Hissmann, MPIV Seewiesen, p. 46; © Jürgen Schauer, MPIV Seewiesen, p. 48; © IPS/Cynthia Zemlicka, p. 49 (both); © Pieter Venter, pp. 59, 60; © Tony Arruza/CORBIS, p. 62.

SELECTED BIBLIOGRAPHY

As I gathered and interpreted information about coelacanths from books and journals, I came across numerous questions that could be answered only by specialists. Years ago, when I began writing books, contacting those scientists would have meant sending a flurry of letters all over the world, then waiting weeks for a response. Fortunately for my research, electronic mail has transformed scholarship in the past decade. Mark Erdmann, Karen Hissmann, and Robin Stobbs were able to respond to my many inquiries within hours rather than weeks. That said, convenience isn't everything. Receiving a much-hoped-for letter from Marjorie Courtenay-Latimer, mailed all the way from South Africa to Illinois in response to a letter of my own, was a thrill I won't forget.

Even with the help of specialists, I found I had to accept that many coelacanth questions simply haven't been answered yet. After years of study, scientists are still uncertain how the rostral organ works, how coelacanths capture prey, and where pups live, among other puzzles. Those of us who aren't fortunate enough to be a Trimix diver in Sodwana Bay or a submersible scientist in the Comoro Islands must rely on the scientists of the future to find new evidence—and, of course, new questions.

While we wait, those who wish to learn more about coelacanths might want to read Samantha Weinberg's *A Fish Caught in Time: The Search for the Coelacanth* (HarperCollins, 2000). This outstanding book fleshes out the personal as well as the scientific dramas of the coelacanth quests in a vibrant, fascinating way. Published prior to the South Africa discoveries of 2000 and 2001, it is the most detailed account I've seen of the coelacanth story to that point. My work benefited greatly from both Weinberg's research and her generous answers to my questions.

I also recommend J. L. B. Smith's *Old Fourlegs: The Story of the Coelacanth* (Longmans, Green and Co., 1956), which remains a readable, suspenseful account of Smith's achievements and dogged commitment to his obsession. It's also a wonderful snapshot of how science was conducted and publicized during the 1950s. (American readers may have better luck locating this book under the title *The Search Beneath the Sea;* both editions are sadly out of print.) These and other works that I think young readers would find appealing are noted below with an asterisk (*), within a selected bibliography of additional books, periodicals, and websites I consulted.

BOOKS

Forey, Peter. *History of the Coelacanth Fishes.* Boca Raton, FL: Chapman & Hall, 1997.

*Long, John A. *The Rise of Fishes: 500 Million Years of Evolution.* Baltimore: Johns Hopkins University Press, 1995.

SELECTED BIBLIOGRAPHY CONTINUED

McCosker, John E., and Michael D. Lagios, eds. *Biology and Physiology of the Living Coelacanth.* San Francisco: California Academy of Sciences, 1979.

*Smith, J. L. B. *Old Fourlegs: The Story of the Coelacanth.* London: Longmans, Green and Co., 1956.

Thomson, Keith S. *Living Fossil: The Story of the Coelacanth.* New York: W. W. Norton and Co., 1991.

*Weinberg, Samantha. *A Fish Caught in Time: The Search for the Coelacanth.* New York: HarperCollins, 2000.

PERIODICALS

*Courtenay-Latimer, Marjorie. "Reminiscences of the Discovery of the Coelacanth, *Latimeria Chalumnae* Smith." *Cryptozoology* 8 (1988): 1–11.

Environmental Biology of Fishes 23 (1991). (Entire volume devoted to coelacanth studies.)

Erdmann, Mark. "An Account of the First Living Coelacanth Known to Scientists from Indonesian Waters." *Environmental Biology of Fishes* 54 (1999): 439–443.

——. "Indonesian 'King of the Sea' Discovered." *Nature* 395 (Sept. 24, 1998): 335.

*Fricke, Hans. "Coelacanths: The Fish That Time Forgot." *National Geographic* 173 (June 1988): 824–838.

——, and Karen Hissmann. "Feeding Ecology and Evolutionary Survival of the Living Coelacanth *Latimeria Chalumnae.*" *Marine Biology* 136 (2000): 379–386.

——, and Karen Hissmann. "Locomotion, Fin Coordination, and Body Form of the Living Coelacanth." *Environmental Biology of Fishes* 34 (1992): 331–333.

——, and Karen Hissmann. "Natural Habitat of Coelacanths." *Nature* 346 (July 1990): 323–324.

Pouyaud, Laurent. "A New Species of Coelacanth." *Life Sciences* 322 (1999): 261–267.

Schauer, Jürgen, et. al. "A Method of Deployment of Externally Attached Sonic Fish Tags from a Manned Submersible and Their Effects on Coelacanths." *Marine Biology* 128 (1997): 359–362.

Smith, J. L. B. "A Living Coelacanthid Fish from South Africa." *Transactions of the Royal Society of South Africa* 28 (1940).

——. "A Living Fish of Mesozoic Type." *Nature* (March 1939): 455–456.

WEBSITES

Coelacanth: The Fish Out of Time
   <http://www.dinofish.com>

Coelacanths on Stamps
   <http://www.members.tripod.com/~Coelastamp/>

Sulawesi Coelacanth, University of California-Berkeley
   <http://www.ucmp.berkeley.edu/vertebrates/coelacanth/coelacanths.html>

GLOSSARY

BASILAR PAPILLA (BA-zih-luhr puh-PIH-lah): a membrane found in the ears of coelacanths and some animals that hear in air, such as mammals and some amphibians. Among fishes, only the coelacanth has this membrane.

CARTILAGE (KAR-tuh-lidge): flexible, rubbery tissue that makes up a coelacanth's notochord

DENTICLES: toothlike spines found on the scales of some fishes

DEVONIAN PERIOD: a period of time between approximately 360 and 410 million years ago. Called the "Age of Fishes," the Devonian period saw the evolution of many new fishes, including coelacanths.

DNA: material found in the cells of all living things that carries the pattern of characteristics parents pass to their offspring. DNA stands for deoxyribonucleic acid.

EPICAUDAL FIN: an extension of the caudal fin, or tail fin, of a coelacanth. The coelacanth is the only modern fish with an epicaudal fin.

GENUS: in scientific classification, a group of animals or plants that are alike in certain ways

LOBED: rounded. A lobed fin is rounded and fleshy, unlike the rayed fins that most fishes have, which are slender and are supported by thin spines.

MISSING LINK: an organism that, if found, would bridge a gap in scientists' understanding of the theory of evolution. Scientists have debated whether the coelacanth may be the missing link between fish and amphibians—the first fish to evolve legs and walk on land.

NOTOCHORD (NOH-tuh-kord): a flexible, tubelike structure that supports a coelacanth's body

OTOLITHS (OH-tuh-liths): ear bones that can be measured to reveal a coelacanth's age

OVOVIVIPAROUS (OH-voh-vye-VIH-puh-ruhs): bearing young that grow inside eggs within the mother's body, then hatch and continue developing within the mother before birth

RETINA: the part of the eye that senses and reacts to light

ROSTRAL ORGAN: a large, jelly-filled sac located in a coelacanth's head cavity and connected to six tubes that open on either side of the fish's snout. Unique to coelacanths, the rostral organ is believed to be a sensory organ.

SPECIES: a type of animal or plant. Members of the same species can mate and produce young that look like themselves.

SWIM BLADDER: an organ that some fishes use to regulate their depth in the water

TAPETUM (tuh-PEE-tuhm): a layer of cells within the eyes of some animals that reflects light

VERTEBRATE (VUHR-tuh-bruht): an animal with a backbone. While most vertebrates have a spinal cord made up of bony vertebrae, a coelacanth has just a notochord.

INDEX

Numbers in **bold** type refer to photographs or illustrations.